Praise for

HOPELIFTER

"To 'lift up' is to raise or direct something upward. As you read *Hopelifter*, you will be inspired in powerful and practical ways, for God greatly desires to use *you* to lift hope to those around you. And as they look upward, they may just meet Jesus, our Living Hope!"

— MARLAE GRITTER, Executive Vice President
of Moms in Prayer International

"Full of powerful, sometimes gut-wrenching stories, this inspirational book made me want to shout, "I want to be a hopelifter! Here I am, Lord, use me!" Thanks to Kathe Wunnenberg and several other contributors for delivering such a practical, hands-on resource for those who want to be Jesus to the hurting."

— CHERI KEAGGY, Dove Award-winning
singer/songwriter/speaker and fellow hopelifter

"Kathe Wunnenberg is an extravagant Hopelifter. For years I have watched Kathe mobilize the resources of heaven and earth to help hurting people. She sees divine possibilities. Her book *Hopelifter* is brimming with tangible ways to put hope into action. Read it and catch this contagious vision. Be a hopelifter!"

— ANNE DENMARK, President,
Life Discovery Coaching

Other Books by Kathe Wunnenberg

Grieving the Child I Never Knew

Grieving the Loss of a Loved One

Longing for a Child

HOPELIFTER

CREATIVE WAYS TO SPREAD HOPE
WHEN LIFE HURTS

KATHE
WUNNENBERG

ZONDERVAN

Hopelifter
Copyright © 2013 by Kathe Wunnenberg

This title is also available as a Zondervan ebook. Visit www.zondervan.com/ebooks.

This title is also available in a Zondervan audio edition. Visit www.zondervan.fm.

Requests for information should be addressed to:
Zondervan, *Grand Rapids, Michigan 49530*

Library of Congress Cataloging-in-Publication Data

Wunnenberg, Kathe.
    Hopelifter : creative ways to spread hope when life hurts / Kathe Wunnenberg.
       p. cm.
    Includes bibliographical references.
    ISBN 978-0-310-32015-9 (pbk.)
       1. Christian women — Religious life. 2. Hope — Religious aspects — Christianity.
    I. Title.
    BV4527.W85 2013
    248.8'43 — dc23   2013010445

Cover design: Curt Diepenhorst
Cover Photo: Shutterstock®
Interior illustration: Shutterstock®
Interior design: Beth Shagene

Printed in the United States of America

13 14 15 16 17 18 19 /DCI/ 22 21 20 19 18 17 16 15 14 13 12 11 10 9 8 7 6 5 4 3 2 1

This book is lovingly dedicated to:

God, You are the Creator of my hope and future
Jesus, my Hopelifter,
Without you, I have no hope
Holy Spirit, You are the Power behind my hope
And
To you, the reader
You are the one who spreads hope

CONTENTS

*RECIPES OF HOPE TOPICS

ACKNOWLEDGMENTS

This book is about being a hopelifter and spreading hope to hurting people. I am grateful to those who supported me as hopelifters in this journey for a reason or season to make this book a reality. I applaud each of you for doing your part to be the hands and heart of Jesus to me. Together, we did it!

My PIT Team: Alice, Donna, Nancy, Brenda, Debbie, Lisa, Anne, Marlae, Rhonda, Louise, Karen, Adrienne, Kim, Erica, Becky, Judy, DD, Lori, Karen, Debbie, Gloria, and Leanne. Without you and the power behind you, I never would have made it! Your prayers lifted me and helped me persevere. What a journey of miracles we experienced!

Cindy Lambert: Thank you for catching the vision for this book many years ago and sharing the vision with Zondervan in God's perfect timing. Thanks also for your friendship and for persevering beyond your call of duty to help create the perfect subtitle.

My Zondervan Family:

Executive acquisitions editor Carolyn McCready: Your gracious spirit and willingness to step in and oversee this project inspired me.

Freelance editor Lori Vanden Bosch: Thanks for putting the puzzle together. You stretched me and helped me grow.

Senior editor at large Verlyn Verbrugge: Thanks for your finishing touches and for helping me connect to "Joy" again.

Creative director Michelle Lenger: I love your "spreading like wildflowers" cover design.

Composition staff Sarah Johnson and Beth Shagene: Thanks for putting the pages together so elegantly.

Senior Director of Marketing, Tom Dean: Thank you for your marketing support and allowing me to pray for rain.

My Family:

Rich, Jake, Josh and Jordan: Thanks for being the men in my life who did laundry, drove, cooked, cleaned, and did your part to support me so I could write.

Mom: Thank you for your prayers and for reading every page of my manuscript.

Dad: Thank you for sharing a possession—the pictures of Crystal's wedding.

Danny and Lethia: Thank you for sharing a place of hope for me to be inspired and write—Aunt Kat's Bed and Breakfast in Marquand, Missouri.

My Project Managers:

Adam Colwell Write Works: Thanks for managing the submissions for Recipes of Hope.

Louve Notes Media: Mikaela, thanks for your marketing management.

My Project Assistants: Kimberly Bathea and Debbie Mis: Your support in handling the details gave me hope and time to write.

My Story Contributors: Thank you for allowing me to share your personal story or for writing your recipe of hope.

My Hopelifers' Writers Retreat Group: You cheered me on. Many of you are now published!

My Strategy and Marketing Team: Isha Cogborn, Lori Diab, and D D Kuhlman. Your part made a difference.

My Hopelifters Before Me: Jesus, Joshua Tien, Jennie Young, Alice Stephens, Jan Mize, Dr. Michael Tucker, Gene and Carol Kent, Judith Couchman, Marlae Gritter, Cheryl Sacks, Sandy Austin, Nancy Tucker, JoAnne Sullins, Carol Travilla, Holly DelHousaye,

Anne Denmark, Nancy Ray, Mama Afman, and the Speak Up Staff, and Moms in Prayer International, thank you for leading the way.

My Hopelifters Beside Me:
My friends in the fire for a season: Lisa Jernigan, Jan James, and CBWA.

My friends who offered presence, words, calls, or texts for reasons or seasons: Debbie Mis, Brenda Dull, Lisa Kowalski, Darlene Adams, Donna Morris, Karen Ray, Leanne Gregory, Kris Durfee, Mary Jane Farr, and Diane Markins.

My Hopelifters Behind Me: All of you who have shared your hurts with me for a moment, a day, or a season who are in the process of hope. You are the next generation of hopelifters.

My Ministry Partners:
Gia Chapman, Shayla VanHofwegen, Kim Slaughter, and Debbie Kennedy: Thank you for partnering our ministries together to spread hope to grieving moms.

Living Water Retreat Center: Thank you for providing a place of hope and healing to experience God's transforming power.

Master's Touch Tours: Thanks Warren, Debbie, and Ernie for bus trips that heal broken hearts.

My Make-Over Specialists: Sandra Saoud of Sincerely Sandra: Thank you for transforming my face when I was sick, for my picture, and for decades of friendship.

Sherry Drolet of Totally Transformed: Your vision to transform a media room into an inspirational writing space to write this book was amazing!

Sophia Roitman Trillo and Cayla Smith: Thanks for your creative help behind the scenes.

My Baristas at Frys (40th and Ray): Thanks for handing me venti hope in a cup each writing day.

FOREWORD

The phone rang in the middle of the night. My husband picked up the receiver. I looked at the clock. It was 12:35 a.m. Glancing at Gene, I saw a look of shock and horror on his face. He pulled the receiver away from his ear and said, "Jason has just been arrested for the murder of his wife's first husband. He's in the jail in Orlando."

I had never been in shock before. Nausea swept over me. I tried to get out of bed, but my legs wouldn't hold my weight. Our son, a graduate of the U.S. Naval Academy, had married a previously married woman with two little girls. There were multiple allegations of abuse against the biological father of the girls, and he was trying to get unsupervised visitation. As Jason's fears for the girls increased, our son unraveled mentally, emotionally, and spiritually, and he did the unthinkable. He shot and killed a man in a public parking lot and was eventually convicted of first-degree murder.

I was hopeless and desperate. Our hearts were grieving for the family of the deceased and for our son, knowing his future would be far different than anticipated. The financial impact of Jason's criminal defense was devastating. I had made my living as a Christian public speaker, and I had no idea if I would ever be asked to speak again. I was afraid to be seen in public because I didn't know who knew my secret. It was hard to just keep breathing.

Then came an email from my friend Kathe Wunnenberg. She has a heart of compassion like few people I've ever met. Kathe and two other friends got together and asked if they could begin sending out a monthly email update to our family members and friends, informing them of specific prayer requests and tangible needs. We were used to being on the giving end of compassion, and it was hard to admit how much we needed help, but we said yes.

For the next two and a half years, through seven postponements of our son's trial, these remarkable people sent cards and notes of encouragement. Sometimes there were monetary gifts to help with legal expenses, gift cards for groceries, or packages of Kleenex, to remind us that it was okay to cry. Their unique ways of meeting our needs were filled with creativity, love, and prayer. It was an experience of being carried by others when we couldn't carry ourselves.

No one is more qualified to write this book than Kathe Wunnenberg. Her multiple losses and life challenges have equipped her to know what's most needed when people are hurting. *Hopelifter* will challenge you to be intentional about being the hands and feet of Jesus to those in need. But more than that, you will discover "Recipes of Hope," which will give you a hands-on reference tool that will fill you with workable ideas for spreading hope everywhere it's needed.

The principles in this book could become a movement that touches lives with God's inexhaustible resources when life turns out differently from what's anticipated. It starts with one person who says, "I'm available." I challenge you to be that person!

CAROL KENT, Speaker and Author
When I Lay My Isaac Down (NavPress)
Between a Rock and a Grace Place (Zondervan)

PART ONE

DISCOVERING HOPE

CHAPTER 1

HOPELIFTERS HOPE ON WHEELS

Praise be to the God and Father of our Lord Jesus Christ, the Father of compassion and the God of all comfort, who comforts us in all our troubles, so that we can comfort those in any trouble with the comfort we ourselves receive from God.
—2 CORINTHIANS 1:3–4

Take a busload of women away for a day with God!

What a crazy thought. At that time in 2006, I was on a personal retreat seeking rest, replenishment, and direction from God. My life was busy and full. I was struggling to balance marriage, parenting three sons (ages five, seven, and sixteen), a speaking and writing ministry, and a growing new organization called Hopelifters. How could I possibly find the time or energy to organize a bus trip?

But when I shared the idea with my friend Debbie Mis, to my surprise, she got excited. So we spent a day researching bus companies, and Debbie made a notebook to organize the information. Debbie loves details and organization. I lose things. She finds them. Our friendship is truly a gift from God.

Prayer is foundational in anything I do, so Debbie and I prayed together about taking women away on a bus. We prayed specifically for a Christian bus company.

Four years passed.

One day while cleaning out a closet, I found the notebook Debbie had created for me years earlier with the title *Hopelifters Hope on Wheels* on the front. *Now's the time for the bus trip!* I thought. Though sometimes I get frustrated with myself and question my big dreams or ability to realize them, I'm learning to embrace the truth that God's ways and timing are different than mine. His timing is always perfect. I realized this a few days later when I received an unexpected call from Master's Touch Tours, a Christian-owned bus company. Debbie and I met with the owners, and by the end of the meeting I had chartered our first bus to take women away for a day with God.

However, I now faced two obstacles. First, I didn't have the money. And second, I didn't have women for the bus trip! But one thing I've learned in my life is that when God asks me to do something, even if it doesn't make sense (as long as it's not contrary to Scripture), then JUST DO IT!

I prayed hard. Every day, I asked God to show me who to invite, and every day He led me to women in need of fresh hope, many of them strangers. Then I sensed I was to make my first bus trip an offering and not charge women to attend. Another crazy thought. A few friends heard about my bus trip and couldn't attend, but felt prompted to underwrite some of the expense, so God even provided most of the funds.

March 2010 finally arrived, and thirty-three women ranging from ages thirteen to eighty-one arrived for an early morning breakfast and boarded the bus for a two-hour ride to Living Water Retreat Center. From my personal experience of going there, I understood the value of removing myself physically from my environment and releasing my emotions, so that my spirit could be still enough to hear God. I looked forward to providing this opportunity to other women. Together, Debbie and I served women that day and watched the Holy Spirit at work through their laughter, life-to-life exchange, tears, praise, healing, and changed hearts.

We continue to make it a practice to take women away on a bus for the day to spend intentional time with God and experience His transforming power. We call our day trips "Hopelifters Hope on Wheels." Hope spreads as women on the bus reach out to other women in need of hope. This intentional lifestyle, which I call *hopelifting, is for anyone who wants to make a difference in hurting lives and spread the hope and comfort of God through creative compassion — simple, practical, creative acts. Hope is contagious. It is carried from person to person and is transmitted by contact.* Our bus trip is simply a venue for a life-giving transfusion of hope.

A Busload of Grieving Moms

"All aboard!" shouts Ernie, our bus driver. Ernie's warmth, humor, and experience as a former grief pastor always enhances our Mother's Day bus trip and makes our two-hour drive from Phoenix to Living Water Retreat Center a meaningful experience. This particular bus trip is dear to my heart, because it is for women who have lost children. Each mother there represents a life and a unique circumstance: unborn children lost through abortion, miscarriage, or stillbirth. Infants lost through premature birth, rare disorders, or unknown causes. Young children and teenagers lost through accidents, sickness, or suicide. Adult children lost through murder, accidents, or health issues.

Although the women's ages, stages in life, and grief vary, they share a common bond and sisterhood of loss. Some are fresh in their journey and preparing for their first Mother's Day without their child. Others are veteran sojourners, well familiar with suffering and this bus trip. We call them hopelifters — *people who have been transformed by their own experience with grief and who are now willingly offering themselves as the hands and feet of Jesus to comfort other hurting women.* Amazingly, God's power at work in and through their broken hearts spreads hope in the hearts of others. I've seen it happen every year. The hopelifters' presence, personal touch, prayers, practical advice, and individual stories of God's help and healing power in their own lives lifts other women and points them to the God of Hope. And in time ... those receiving hope will spread hope too.

As the emcee and spiritual tour guide for the trip, I stood up and faced the two long rows of women. On one side sat many brokenhearted women in need of knowing Jesus personally or knowing He is with them in their pain. Across the aisle in the other row sat the hopelifters, women persevering through their pain yet willing to help others.

"Welcome!" I said. "I'm glad you are on today's bus, but I'm

> *We believe we go through what we go through to help others go through what we went through.*

sorry for your loss. Many of us are here today because we believe we go through what we go through, to help others go through what we went through." Unlike other bus trips I emcee for hurting women who need a day away with God, today's busload of grieving moms is one of my favorites because I share in their suffering and know what it feels like to lose a child. I also know how God's miracle-working power can transform lives and bring healing, hope, and freedom.

On the bus, women are encouraged to be real and share their raw emotions or feelings with no judgment from others. Women may choose to be silent or choose to share pictures or stories of their lost child. Passing the microphone for "show and tell" is another meaningful way for women to express their joy or sorrow.

"I don't know if God is even there," sobbed one woman that day. "I'm going crazy trying to figure out why this happened!" said another. "I started a nonprofit ministry this year to honor my twins, and we provide hospitals with boxes filled with meaningful items for women who have lost babies," said another. Then Deborah shared about her loss, her hardened heart toward God, and her severe health challenges. "I have a hip tumor with severe pain and difficulty walking," she announced. As women continued sharing, a sense of camaraderie started to develop. By the time we reached our destination and the bus pulled into the gravel driveway of the lush thirty-acre retreat center, women knew they were not alone.

Finding Hope and Healing

During our lunch program in the dining hall, a few women shared their personal stories and how their faith helped them endure their loss. "Without God, I couldn't make it." Nodding heads affirmed the speaker's message.

After lunch I encouraged women to spend the afternoon with God and to enjoy a prayer walk created for them. "Follow the butterfly balloons," I said. One stop led women to a large metal cross in the middle of a field with a flowing fountain. Surrounding the cross and fountain was a square, concrete-base seating area. I enjoy sitting at the base of this wilderness cross listening to the soothing water. Sometimes I pour out my heart to God, while other times I reflect on the words, "For God so loved the world that He gave His one and only Son, that whoever believes in Him shall not perish but have eternal life" (John 3:16). I try to imagine Jesus being lifted up, to suffer and die for my sin on a cross so that I can have eternal hope. Jesus, the ultimate Hopelifter.

Later that afternoon, I met with Deborah after her stop at the cross. She was upset, but I sensed God was at work. After listening to her pour out her questions and pain, I simply asked, "Do you want to be healed from your anguish?"

Surprised by my question, she paused, thought for a moment, then nodded.

"Has anyone ever prayed for you about this?" I asked.

"No," she said.

"Would you be willing to receive prayer today at the pond at our closing session?" I asked.

"Yes," she said.

As women gathered by the tree-lined pond for our late afternoon time of personal sharing, praise, and thanksgiving, I was amazed by how the mood had changed since earlier that day on the bus. Most were smiling and laughing. New friendships had formed. I listened as woman after woman shared how God showed up in personal ways that day. We thanked God together for the hope and healing.

Then I invited Deborah to come forward. I asked the others to surround her and join me in a circle of praise to acknowledge God for who He is. "God, You are powerful." "You are good." "You are faithful to Deborah." "God, I praise You for being Deborah's hope and healer." "You are her strength and truth." "You are the God who transforms her." "You are her life and freedom." "You are her Hopelifter."

We ended our time with a Jordan crossing, a signature activity of most Hopelifter events. With the pond as the backdrop, I read the story from Joshua 3:1–18 of the Israelites facing the flooded Jordan River and crossing over on dry ground.

Then I called the hopelifters forward, the women who had poured out their hope that day to hurting women, and asked them to stand with me and face the others. To me, they symbolized the priests from the Jordan crossing, leading the way by lifting up God and pointing others to Him.

When we lift God up, He parts the water and crosses us over to a new place of hope.

"When we lift God up, He parts the water and crosses us over to a new place of hope. Are you ready to cross over?" I asked.

Our group of hopelifters led the others in a symbolic "Jordan crossing" walk around the pond. Then I shared from Joshua 4 how the Israelites took rocks from the dry riverbed and built a memorial on the bank as a reminder of God's miracle-working power to enable them to cross the Jordan River on dry ground. Instead of rocks, we handed each woman a colorful magnetic butterfly, a reminder of God's transforming power and how He personally encouraged each woman that day.

Deborah's Miracle

A few days later I received a call from Deborah. "Kathe, I just met with my doctor and was told my hip tumor is gone."

I nearly dropped the phone. Although I know God still performs physical healing, I was not expecting this good news. I asked Deborah to send me an email and to give me her permission to share her good news with others from the bus.

Here is what she wrote:

Hi Kathe,

I hope you had a great Mother's Day—I sure did! I am still celebrating the good news I received on Friday. The doctor's office called me with the results of my repeat CT with more specific views. When she called, she informed me I no longer needed to worry because the tumor is GONE! Not smaller, different, changed, or anything else—just gone.

Praise the Lord! I know it was the prayers of the wonderful women I was with along with the Holy Spirit that loved us the whole day. Thank you for the wonderful day! Thanks to the women who prayed for me! Thanks to our Lord who healed me! God is good! I also spoke at church on Mother's Day about how the Lord has transformed my life and filled it with joy! I was able to speak to my church family without tears— what a wonderful feeling! Still smiling.

Love,
Deborah

Over the next few days I heard more stories of God's transforming power from women on the bus trip. When I see my butterfly magnet on my refrigerator, I'm reminded of that bus trip and how God parted the water of hopelessness, despair, guilt, and disease and crossed women over to the promised land of healing and hope. I can hardly wait for future bus trips to see transformed women like Deborah spreading hope to a new group of hurting women.

Spreading Hope to Hurting People

This book, like our bus trips, is a living testimony to God's miracle-working power to transform lives, changing the broken and hurting to the hope-filled and helpful—and to the hopelifters, those who spread hope in creative ways. Through these pages we'll explore timeless principles, personal insights, stories, and practical ideas to help you in your journey to spread hope to hurting people in simple or extravagant ways. My favorite part of the book is the Recipes of Hope section written by fellow hopelifters, who have persevered through various life issues and are willing to share their insights to help you encourage others who may be experiencing a similar life struggle. I hope you are encouraged by their creative ideas.

Although you probably picked up this book to help others, don't be surprised if you find hope and healing in the pages for yourself. Like the women on my bus trips, I invite you to bring along your hurts and disappointments and to expect to encounter a mighty God whose power and creativity is limitless. My prayer is that He will meet you personally wherever you are and ignite you with fresh per-spective, passion, purpose, and personal creativity to be the hands, feet, and heart of Jesus. His hope is contagious!

Are you ready to journey with me to spread hope to hurting people? You don't need to join a bus trip to become a hopelifter. All you need is a willing heart and ready hands and feet.

All aboard!

CHAPTER 2

KNOWING HOPE

Guide me in Your truth and teach me,
for You are God my Savior,
and my hope is in You all day long.
—PSALM 25:5

I was running late to an appointment. To make matters worse, traffic on the freeway was stopped as far as I could see. *I'll never make it,* I thought. Frustrated and feeling out of control, I looked up and saw the following words on a bumper sticker in front of me:

No hope?
Know Hope.

These timely words shouted truth to my anxious heart. They reminded me to look beyond my seemingly hopeless situation to the God of hope. During the next several minutes my car became a sanctuary where I communed with God, my Father and the giver of hope. I thanked God for loving me and caring about every concern in my life, even a traffic jam. To my surprise, I looked around and felt compassion for the other frustrated drivers. What hurts were they experiencing? What needs did they have? As I continued to wait, I prayed for them.

That day I experienced a fresh awareness that hurting people are all around us and opportunities abound daily for us to help others. But before reaching out, we need to first know the history of hope, what hope is, and the God of hope, to fully understand how to give it.

History of Hope

The first time *hope* is mentioned in the Bible is by Naomi, saying to her daughters-in-law that there was no hope of her having more sons. I can only imagine the deep sorrow Naomi must have felt after losing her husband, her two married sons, and her hope for future family. To her surprise her daughter-in-law Ruth chose to leave her family, worship Naomi's God, and follow Naomi to her homeland. What a precious gift of presence and personal sacrifice Ruth gave to Naomi. Two widows sojourning together, starting over in a new land. Guided by Naomi's wisdom and coaching, Ruth was eventually blessed with a new husband and a son.

Can you picture the first time Naomi held her new grandson? As she touched his tiny fingers and counted his miniature toes, did she marvel at the miracle of hope birthed again in her heart? Was she giddy with excitement and awe? As she celebrated, the other women said, "Praise be to the LORD, who this day has not left you without a guardian-redeemer. May he become famous throughout Israel! He will renew your life and sustain you in your old age. For your daughter-in-law, who loves you and who is better to you than seven sons, has given him birth" (Ruth 4:14–15). Amazingly, Naomi's grandson became the grandfather of David, the king of Israel.

Can you think of a time in your past when a circumstance seemed hopeless, but God finally revealed His hope to you or through someone? The story of Ruth and Naomi reminds us to trust God and know His hope even when circumstances appear to have no hope. While our story may appear hopeless now, often later on we can look back on history (His Story!) and discover God's plan at work in our lives during that time.

Hope Defined

In the Old Testament, the word "hope" most often invites us to look ahead eagerly with trust and confident expectation. It also reminds us that the fulfillment of hope lies in the future. Lawrence Richards notes, "As the centuries drifted by, the prophets revealed more and

more of God's plan. The shape of the hoped-for futur
clearer and clearer form ... Despite sharpening images o
to take place in the near and distant future, the Old Testament never
shifts from the conviction that relationship with God is the ultimate
ground of hope. It is God himself who is the hope of Israel (Jeremiah
14:8; 17:13). It is only by focusing our gaze on Him that we find a
source of confidence and patience."[1]

Hope is found in God's Word. God trusted Moses with His words
on the mountain. He wrote them down on stone tablets and presented them to the people as the Ten Commandments to guide the
people in how to live. His Word, placed in the ark of the covenant,
led the Israelites from slavery in Egypt, through
the desert for forty years, and into the Promised
Land. Multitudes still follow the Bible, God's
Word, and find hope, truth, joy, and guidance
for daily living.

> *Hope is not wishful thinking, but trusting God Himself and what He has promised.*

Hope is not wishful thinking, but trusting
God Himself and what He has promised. Larry
Richards points out, "Literally hundreds of
times the phrase 'the word of Yahweh' is found
in the Old Testament, and there are hundreds
more that speak of God's sending his word to
his people ... The Old Testament shines with
confidence that every word from God is both reliable and relevant."[2]
The psalmist pours out his heart to remind us to find rest in God,
seek Him, hope in Him, and put our hope in His Word. Listen to his
words: "My soul faints with longing for Your salvation, but I have
put my hope in Your word" (Psalm 119:81).

God's Word spoken, read, or sung can change our mind-set,
mood, and behavior. It teaches, corrects, admonishes, and encourages
us. In a world of lies and deception, it points us to truth and absolutes.

Hope in God

"Curse God and die!"

These were not the words Job expected to hear from his wife

(Job 2:9) during a time when he needed comfort and hope after losing his children, possessions, and health. Pain is personal and sometimes can bring out the fears and flaws in people. Hurt people often hurt people. Job's wife was suffering too, yet her response to it was much different than her husband's. Thankfully, Job ignored her words, yet I wonder if he ever forgot them. He was real and honest with his pain.

Life had lost all meaning for Job. *What have I done to deserve what has happened?* Job wondered. Tormented by doubts and uncertainties, Job cried out in anguish. Surely his closest friends would know how to offer him hope.

To his disappointment Job's friends hurled insults, theology, and answers to why God was punishing him. They wrongfully accused and misunderstood Job. Suffering people need supportive friends who will validate their pain and simply offer the gift of presence and unconditional love. Do you remember a time when you needed support from a friend and they disappointed you?

I love Job's persevering faith. Even though his wife and friends let him down, he continued to trust God. "Though He slay me, yet I will hope in Him" (Job 13:15).

Job's longsuffering and patience endured through pain and uncertainty. When God finally spoke to Job, He did not humiliate or condemn him, but neither did He explain why He allowed Job to suffer. In talking with Job, God acknowledged Job's righteousness, but at the same time God pointed Job toward His greatness and His mystery. Job did not know, as the reader does, that Job was a key figure in a battle between God and Satan, with Satan accusing Job of being righteous just because he was blessed. Job's righteousness even in the midst of his suffering proved Satan wrong, and honored God.

Job's life encourages us to trust in God even when we are suffering. If we bow before Him, we can find hope in God's greatness and goodness even when we cannot understand either our suffering or God himself and what He is doing. Like Job, we may be unaware of a spiritual battle going on behind the scenes, but we can rest in the hope that God is good, God is in control, and God has a purpose and a plan.

Hope in Action

During an extreme season of personal and family suffering, I questioned why God would allow more painful circumstances in my life. I was dealing with parenting issues and a son's health challenges shortly after persevering through the loss of a ministry, a major transition in our church, the death of a personal dream, and the death of our infant son. Overall, I believed I had "suffered well" and modeled a positive, authentic, hope-filled faith through every situation, allowing each experience to enlarge me and be used to help others. I was intentional about spreading hope and saw evidence of fruitfulness through a new ministry, three books, and many transformed people.

Why *more* suffering? I wondered.

Is a time of peace and calm too much to ask of God?

Like Job, I wrestled with tormenting thoughts and emotions. Was I suffering from the consequences of my sin or bad decisions? Had I disobeyed or displeased God? Were spiritual forces targeting my family?

Physically exhausted from fighting doubt, uncertainty, and disappointment, I longed for rest and replenishment. I isolated myself from others, afraid to overburden them with the multiple challenges I was facing. I cried out to God. No explanation came. Yet, in the midst of His silence, He whispered His love through friends He sent to comfort me.

One friend whisked me away for twenty-four hours. Her carefully laid plans included a night's stay at a friend's home who was out of town. When we arrived she handed me a book on the twenty-third psalm, a journal, and a basket of my favorite things.

"Take a long, hot shower, relax, and spend time with God!" she said. Then she left me alone for the afternoon.

Unlike Job's friends, who tried to give reasons for his suffering and hurled accusations at him, my friend comforted me by not asking questions. Instead of reprimanding me for not returning her phone calls, she served me. She planned a surprise game night with a group of friends, gave me laughter, and expected nothing in return.

A few days later another friend gave me an inspirational music CD with God's Word. My soul soared with more hope as I listened and heard the melodious truth. Another friend handed me a red afghan to remind me that God is my comforter.

Looking back now, I am convinced that God allowed me to suffer so He could display His warm sense of presence and love through friends. They made it bearable and pointed me to "Know Hope" again.

Know Hope, Show Hope

As you ready yourself to show hope to hurting people, remember to first stop and pray to know the God of hope. Remember the story of Ruth and Naomi and how God eventually restored hope even when their circumstances appeared hopeless. Patiently wait for a revelation of what God is doing and follow Him step by step, as Ruth did when she followed Naomi back to her home.

Next, think about the meaning of hope—how can you look eagerly ahead with trust and confident expectation? More importantly, take a moment right now to focus your gaze on God himself, who is your hope. Thank him for loving you and caring about the details in your life. Then look for hope in God's Word. As you read, look for ways God's Word can guide you, teach you, encourage you, and correct you.

Look for hope in God's Word.

If you are going through an extended season of suffering like Job, learn from his life. Patiently endure your suffering as Job did, knowing that while people may let you down, God is great, and God is good, and He has His reasons and purposes even if you can't see them.

Finally, when you endure suffering, look for the ways God shows you hope. Be alert to His comfort from Scripture, song, prayer, or friends. Or if you know someone who is suffering, look for ways to help her know the God of hope. Ultimately, our hope rests not in the end of our suffering, but in God Himself, and especially His Son—as we will see in the next chapter.

CHAPTER 3

HOPE
IN A PERSON

God our Savior and Christ Jesus our hope . . .
—1 TIMOTHY 1:1

*We remember before our God and Father your work pro-
duced by faith, your labor prompted by love, and your
endurance inspired by hope in our Lord Jesus Christ.*
—1 THESSALONIANS 1:3

A young American missionary traveled to China in the 1950s. He went as a teacher, hoping to build relationships to open the door to share the gospel of Jesus Christ. Living alone in a foreign godless country was more difficult than he imagined, and although he enjoyed his work, he felt as if his ministry was failing.

One day he arrived home to discover it had been vandalized and most of his personal belongings destroyed. He suspected the vandals to be the group of teenage boys he had recently met. In desperation and deep sorrow, the missionary dropped to his knees and began to cry out to God. He praised God for being faithful, for being his comforter and his strength. With tears streaming down his face he thanked God for bringing him to China and even for the people who had destroyed his home. As his custom, the missionary began to pray aloud for people, by name.

As he prayed, "God bless Joshua ...," a teenage boy, crouched outside beneath the missionary's open window, jumped to his feet. His curiosity mounted, and he peeked in the window and saw the teacher on his knees. He listened as the man cried out his name repeatedly and asked God to bless him.

Joshua felt strange. Instead of gloating over his deed, he felt ashamed. What puzzled him more was the teacher's response. Joshua couldn't stop thinking about it. A few days later he went to see the teacher. When Joshua went home that day, his heart was transformed, and he had a new friend, Jesus Christ.

The Birth of a Missionary

The teacher mentored Joshua, and one day Joshua announced, "I want to be a missionary like you." With his teacher's support and direction, Joshua moved to the United States and attended seminary. After graduation, Joshua planned to return to China to serve and save his people. Unfortunately the political climate had changed, and Joshua could only return to China if he renounced his faith in Jesus. So Joshua remained in the United States, continued his education, and in the 1960s he became an evangelist traveling the country and conducting revivals.

One of his stops took him to a small country church in a rural Missouri town. One night when Joshua was sharing his story, a seven-year-old girl sat in the audience, listening intently. Although she didn't hear an audible voice, she heard someone whisper to her heart and call *her* name. Without hesitation, she responded in faith and prayed: "Dear Jesus, I need You in my life. I'm a sinner. Please forgive me. I believe You are the Son of God and You came to earth to save me. You suffered and died on a cross for my sins. On the third day You rose from the dead, and You went to heaven to prepare a place for me to live with You forever. Come into my heart, Jesus, be my friend forever."

The little girl bounded home that night to share the good news with her family about Jesus. She hasn't stopped talking about Him since.

Jesus: Our Greatest Hope

I suppose you have figured out that the little girl was me. All those years ago, I had my first encounter with the source and substance of all hope: Jesus Himself. Jesus, the Son of God, was God Himself and was born as a human, yet sinless. Jesus came to be one of us, to walk with us, to relate to us, and to save us from our sin.

Jesus' name means "deliverer" or "savior." He came to earth on a rescue mission to seek and save the spiritually lost. We were helpless and hopeless to save ourselves. As Romans 3:23 tells us, "All have sinned and fall short of the glory of God." We needed a Savior, so God sent Jesus. "For God so loved the world that He gave His one and only Son, that whoever believes in Him shall not perish but have eternal life" (John 3:16). That's good news! Jesus took our place and died for our sins to give us hope and eternal life. We didn't deserve it. We can't earn it. It can only be received by faith. His blood paid the price for everything.

The night I received God's gift of grace as a young girl I remember looking up at a large portrait of Jesus on the church's wall. Jesus is standing outside a door, gently knocking. His eyes, filled with tenderness, appeared as if they were looking directly at me. Although I'd sat in church staring at the portrait countless times, I'd never noticed His eyes before. Yet, in that moment, I knew something had changed. My heart and my perspective were different. Opening the door of my heart to Jesus, my Savior, was the beginning of a new life with Him and His living hope.

Revelation 3:20 says, "Here I am! I stand at the door and knock. If anyone hears My voice and opens the door, I will come in and eat with that person, and they with Me." If you've never received God's gift of grace, you can right now. Salvation and eternity is available to anyone who calls on the name of the Lord (Romans 10:13). Open the door to your heart right now, invite Jesus in, and join Him in living hope.

Jesus, Our Living Hope

"Praise be to the God and Father of our Lord Jesus Christ! In His great mercy He has given us new birth into a living hope through the resurrection of Jesus Christ from the dead" (1 Peter 1:3). Three days after Jesus died on a cross, the tomb was empty. Jesus rose from the grave, paving the way for all who believe in Him to defeat death and enjoy eternal life with Him.

Jesus offers all people hope. Not only hope for life after death and an eternity in heaven, but hope to live a full and meaningful life *now*. John 1:4 says, "In Him was life." The

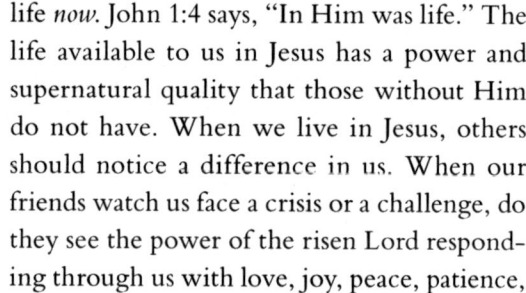

When we live in Jesus, others should notice a difference in us.

life available to us in Jesus has a power and supernatural quality that those without Him do not have. When we live in Jesus, others should notice a difference in us. When our friends watch us face a crisis or a challenge, do they see the power of the risen Lord responding through us with love, joy, peace, patience, kindness, goodness, faithfulness, gentleness, and self-control (see Galatians 5:22–23)? Do our families see the difference Christ makes when we face a need? How has your new birth into the living hope of Jesus changed your life?

In His time here on earth, Jesus not only made it possible for us to experience His hope within us, but He also showed us how to bring that hope to others. If we observe His actions, we can see how He brought hope to the hurting in three major ways. First and most tangibly, He met physical needs. Second, He sensed and met emotional needs. And third, He met spiritual needs. As we seek to bring hope to hurting people, let's consider these three areas—physical, emotional, and spiritual—and act as Jesus' hands and heart in those areas. But first let's take a look at how the Master did it.

Jesus Met Physical Needs

Jesus was a man of compassion. His heart broke for hurting people, and He reached out to bring hope by providing for their basic physical needs like hunger, and also their need for healing from disease, disabilities, and sickness. Matthew tells of a time when "great crowds came to Him, bringing the lame, the blind, the crippled, the mute and many others, and laid them at His feet; and He healed them" (Matthew 15:30). Today, missionaries and countless Christian medical professionals continue to use their time and talents to bring healing to the sick and disabled. And numerous caring people, especially mothers, bring their soothing, healing touch to the ill.

But Jesus doesn't focus on just the "glamorous" miracles of healing. He also remembers the everyday needs of people. After this amazing time of healing, He says to His disciples, "I have compassion for these people; they have already been with me three days and have nothing to eat. I do not want to send them away hungry, or they may collapse on the way" (Matthew 15:32).

Jesus enlisted his disciples to help, and you probably know the rest of the story: Jesus multiplied hope through a few loaves and fish and fed over four thousand people. Matthew says, "They all ate and were satisfied" (15:37), and not only that, but there were baskets full of leftovers! What a wonderful reminder for us to never minimize the importance of meeting a basic need like hunger by bringing a meal to someone who is hurting, busy, or lonely. You may not be able to feed a multitude; however, offer what you can, and see what God will do.

Offer what you can and see what God will do.

Physical needs are some of the easiest needs to spot. As the hands of Jesus on this earth, look for those who are disabled, sick, hungry, or suffering in an obvious way. Then look for tangible ways you can offer help: a bag of groceries, help with chores or errands, a monetary gift, or any other creative ways to show you care.

Jesus Met Emotional Needs

When people suffered, Jesus knew how to meet them where they were in their emotional pain and offered personal support. For example, when Lazarus died, his sister Mary cried out to Jesus, "Lord, if you had been here, my brother would not have died" (John 11:32). When Jesus saw her weeping, "He was deeply moved in spirit and troubled," and He wept (11:33, 35). Although He soon healed Mary's emotional pain by raising Lazarus from the dead, He first stood with her in her time of sorrow, suffering with her.

Some hurts are deeply hidden, but Jesus saw them and addressed them. He reached out to an outcast Samaritan woman, asked her for a drink from a well, then engaged her in conversation. Later, when He asked her to go call her husband, He touched her deepest emotions and helped her see her need for redemption (John 4:16–18).

After Peter realized he had denied Jesus three times during Jesus' time of greatest need, the emotional turmoil he suffered was great. I can only imagine the hope and healing he felt when, after his resurrection, Jesus reached out by asking Peter three times if Peter loved him. Three times Peter said yes, and three times Jesus told him to feed his sheep (John 21:15–17). Jesus helped Peter replace his words of denial with renewed commitment, and He reinstated Peter to his work as a disciple.

Emotional needs are sometimes public, as in the death of a loved one, like Lazarus. But some emotional needs are kept private or are known only to those closest to those who are suffering, as in the case of the Samaritan woman and Peter. Be sensitive to the emotional needs of those around you, bringing Jesus' healing words, acts, and presence to their hearts and spirits. Perhaps a timely word or encouragement through a card or a phone call, a simple gift, a lunch and a listening ear, or even a hug, tissues, or tears would be welcome ways you can soothe an aching heart.

Jesus Met Spiritual Needs

Jesus was a master at meeting spiritual needs. He confronted sinners in need of forgiveness, taught spiritual truth in creative ways, and boldly defeated evil and supernatural forces.

When the woman accused of adultery stood before Jesus, instead of condemning her along with her accusers, He confronted her accusers by writing in the dirt and telling them, "Let any one of you who is without sin be the first to throw a stone at her" (John 8:7). Then, after her accusers left, Jesus spoke privately to the woman and directed her to "go now and leave your life of sin" (8:11). His example encourages us not to condemn and point the finger at sinners, but to confront them in an appropriate and caring way.

Jesus was a master communicator who understood His learners

well. Although His approach, the size of the group, or the setting varied, His goal remained consistent—to bring truth to life and help His followers mature. He mentored the twelve disciples by living with them and teaching them individually, in small groups, and together as a group. Sometimes He preached to multitudes. He often spoke in parables, teaching spiritual truths in creative ways through stories with hidden meaning. He used items His learners could relate to— vines, sheep, seed—to help them grasp truth and apply it to their lives. He embraced every moment, setting, and circumstance as an opportunity to teach a spiritual truth and to mature His followers. His creativity and adaptability inspire me to look for everyday ways to share spiritual truth with people I encounter in a variety of settings.

Jesus also met spiritual needs by defeating evil spiritual forces. The Bible shares several accounts of Jesus healing demon-possessed people, and His authority and power were evident and victorious in every situation. On one occasion the demons possessing a man spoke to Jesus, acknowledged Him as the Son of Most High God, and begged Him not to send them into the abyss but into a herd of pigs instead (Luke 8:26–38). When the man was spiritually healed, Jesus told him, "Return home and tell how much God has done for you" (8:39). When we face the devil and his forces, we need to put on the full armor of God (Ephesians 6:10–18), claiming Jesus' mighty power to defeat evil.

Bringing hope by meeting someone's spiritual need can seem overwhelming. *Isn't that just for pastors to do?* you might think. But Jesus gives us the power and authority to battle evil. He calls us to pray (Ephesians 6:18), to depend on God's Word (6:17), and to speak the gospel fearlessly (6:19). Even a silent, prayerful presence can be a powerful testimony of "God with us" in our suffering.

Hope for a Hurting World

Jesus is our highest hope. He is our Savior and our living hope, for now and all eternity. Others should see a difference in how we live and respond to challenges because of Jesus and His power working in and through us.

> *Jesus is our highest hope. He is our Savior and our living hope, for now and all eternity.*

Jesus was compassionate and brought hope to hurting people by meeting physical, emotional, and spiritual needs. Physical needs are the easiest to spot. Could you offer a meal to a homeless person or a stressed-out single mom? Look for tangible ways to meet needs.

Be sensitive to people who may be suffering emotionally from known situations like a broken relationship or a death. An encouraging word or your offering of tissues or tears could bring hope to a hurting heart. Be aware of silent sufferers, too, those who carry private pain. Could an anonymous gift, a smile, or a hug meet their need?

Bringing spiritual hope to someone may require that you forgive that person or help her recognize her need to give or receive forgiveness. Or it may require you to encourage her to live a new lifestyle without sin. Could you share a timely Scripture or offer your prayer? Be mindful of spiritual forces, put on the full armor of God, and proclaim healing and freedom in Jesus' power, authority, and name. In all these ways, we can be the heart, hands, and feet of Jesus, bringing hope to a hurting world.

CHAPTER 4

THE POWER BEHIND OUR HOPE

Now to Him who is able to do immeasurably more than all we ask or imagine, according to His power that is at work within us, to Him be glory in the church and in Christ Jesus throughout all generations, for ever and ever! Amen.

—EPHESIANS 3:20–21

I walked into the kitchen of Zion House, a home I rented for Hopelifter's annual writer's retreat. The room buzzed with laughter and conversation. I recalled my early years as an aspiring writer attending a similar weekend in Colorado hosted by my friend Judith. Now many years later, it was my season to invest in others. I was energized to help them grow.

To enhance the festive mood, I plopped a bag of popcorn inside the microwave and punched in the cook time. I waited, but nothing happened. I tried again. Still nothing. Finally, after multiple failed attempts, a friend came to my aid. She simply pushed "power" first. Seconds later, I heard *pop, pop, pop.*

Likewise, when we rely on our own strength and effort to help hurting people, we can't produce the results that God fully intends. His power is the Holy Spirit, who is behind our hope and our ability to spread hope to others.

Embracing God's Power

Why does the mere mention of the Holy Spirit make some feel uncomfortable? He's the part of the Trinity most often ignored or misunderstood. Jim Cymbala, author of *Fresh Wind, Fresh Fire*, and pastor of Brooklyn Tabernacle, understands the problem. "Extremists have done fanatical things in the name of the Holy Spirit that have frightened many sincere Christians away,"[3] he says. But Cymbala notes that Satan's tendency is always to push us toward one extreme or the other: deadness or fanaticism. "The old saying is true: 'If you have only the Word, you dry up. If you have only the Spirit, you blow up. But if you have both, you grow up.'"[4]

> *The Holy Spirit is present from the moment you ask Jesus to forgive your sins.*

If you are a believer, the Holy Spirit is present from the moment you ask Jesus to forgive your sins and cleanse your heart. He takes up residence in you. "Don't you know that you yourselves are God's temple and that God's Spirit dwells in your midst?" (1 Corinthians 3:16). We often say that hopelifters are the hands and feet of Christ, but we can only represent Christ to others when His Spirit dwells in us.

How does the Holy Spirit help us as we seek to spread hope? He gives us power. He directs our actions. And He magnifies our efforts.

The Holy Spirit Empowers Us

With only forty days remaining until my book's deadline, I knew the task was humanly impossible to achieve. Life happenings and my overzealous expectations had once again blocked my hope.

"God, please help!"

I shared my challenge during my weekly phone conversation with my life coach, Anne Denmark.

"I've lost my joy!" I spewed. Anne encouraged me to look up the definition of joy. So I grabbed my *Zondervan Expository Dictionary of Bible Words* by Larry Richards. As I scanned the many definitions on the page, my heart leapt. I read these words to Anne over the phone: "Intimate relationship with Jesus is the source of joy ... The believer's joy is produced within, by the Holy Spirit."[5]

I needed this timely reminder that nothing but God could bring me joy.

After several minutes of lively conversation about joy, Anne asked, "What robs you of your joy?"

"Expectations!" I blurted out, then announced, "I'm declaring a 'Nothing but God' fast.

I'm going to fast from human expectations until the book is done."

"Whoo hoo!" cheered Anne.

I'd never heard of this kind of fast, but I knew many people throughout the Bible gave up food for a specific purpose and to deepen their hunger for God. I felt compelled to surrender my human expectations until the book was completed. I was uncertain how to do it, but I wanted joy in my life, and nothing but God could give it.

I stepped forward by asking the Holy Spirit to be my guide and companion. I invited Him to reveal my human expectations and self-effort and to show me truth about my striving or unrest. When I became anxious or driven to achieve, I invited Him to show me "His expectation" through Scripture of how I should overcome a specific challenge. Verses with themes of "surrender," "kindness," "release," "forgiveness," "choose life," "stewardship," and "rest" helped me press on in His strength and joy.

Reliance on the power of the Holy Spirit requires an important step: surrender!

I failed a lot, but I also succeeded. Challenges still happened, but my response to them was different. My fresh awareness of God's promises and power gave me hope. Spreading hope His way, through the power of His strength, to people He knows are hurting, is freeing.

As my writing story shows, reliance on the power of the Holy Spirit requires an important step: surrender!

Put your arms in the air. This simple act communicates "I surrender" and is known globally. If only surrendering to God's authority and control were as easy as throwing our hands up into the air. I'm embarrassed to admit that too many times I've stepped in or spoken up to help someone when I should have surrendered my rights to do or say anything. I've often joked about having "The Messiah Complex"—acting as if I'm the Holy Spirit in someone else's life, guiding them with my thoughts and ways. My husband and three sons will tell you it's true. Needless to say, when I help people in my own strength, it usually hurts them, and I miss God's peace, potential, and power as a hopelifter.

Sometimes I allow my expectations or others' expectations to pressure me into running ahead too soon. I cling to carnality and self-centered ways instead of asking for help and direction. No matter how confident or insecure I may feel about helping someone, I must pause and surrender the person, situation, my plans, resources, and even my prayers to God and invite the Holy Spirit to be my helper. As Paul teaches, "In the same way, the Spirit helps us in our weakness. We do not know what we ought to pray for, but the Spirit himself intercedes for us through wordless groans. And He who searches our hearts knows the mind of the Spirit, because the Spirit intercedes for God's people in accordance with the will of God" (Romans 8:26–27).

Spreading hope to others requires us to have a willingness to embrace the power of His Spirit. Surrender is a continual, never-ending emptying of self. Go ahead. Hands in the air. Release self-effort. Surrender to the Spirit, and you will experience His hope-giving power.

The Holy Spirit Directs Our Actions

Sell your bed on Craigslist.

I tried to dismiss this thought, but couldn't. Although I was reluctant to post information online, fearing scammers or strange people would respond, I felt an urgency to do it anyway.

To my surprise, a woman responded to my posted ad. She told me she and her husband felt prompted by God to move to Arizona. Their long-distance move required them to sell most of their household furniture. That's why they needed a bed for her teenage daughter. The woman's authenticity and frankness about her life and God was refreshing. Despite her inability to pay the full amount for my bed, I felt prompted to invite her to come to see the bed anyway. She agreed. Amazingly, she lived only two miles away.

Later that day, I had the thought, *Give her the bed.*

I knew this familiar voice. *How will my husband receive this directive?* I wondered. Money was tight. I'd already promised him I would use the proceeds from the bed to transform our guest room into a bedroom for our son. When I shared the plan and asked for Rich's blessing, to my surprise and relief, he agreed. "I've learned not to argue with you and God," he chuckled. "Do whatever He says."

I was giddy with excitement as I prepared for my guest's arrival. When the doorbell rang, I welcomed Gloria Bauerle with a hug. She shared more of her story of being a single mom, raising her daughter alone for many years, and the difficult life they had endured. Now a mom of two and happily married to a wonderful Christian man, Gloria realized her oldest daughter had given up on her dream to have a princess bed. "I want her to know dreams can come true," she said.

Then I led her to the guest room. When she saw the four-poster bed draped with white flowing fabric, she said, "This is it! It's the princess bed my daughter has dreamed about."

"God wants you to have it," I said. "Now you can keep your promise to your daughter."

A few days later, a car with a mattress spilling over its roof pulled out of my driveway. This was God's plan to grow a friendship and mentor a leader, speaker, and writer in the making. Little did I know God would use Gloria to make one of my dreams come true, too.

One day Gloria called to tell me she was going on a mission trip to Jordan. She knew I would be excited because I'd always dreamed of going there to see the Jordan River. "I'm making journals to raise my support," she announced.

Buy her journals for your bus, the Spirit whispered. So I put in an order.

Gloria agreed to make journals for all the women on my upcoming Mothers Who Lost Children bus. She needed the money soon, but I didn't have it. Ironically, plans for my garage sale fundraiser were already underway. We agreed Gloria would come after the sale to pick up her money. When I counted the money, I marveled at God's provision: just enough to pay for Gloria's journals. I shared her story of the "Jordan journals" on the bus with broken-hearted moms, and they marveled too. After Gloria returned from her trip, she handed *me* a gift: a small metal chest. When I peeked inside, I was amazed to find three rocks with orange-red dirt in their crevices. "They're your Jordan rocks," she said.

This simple chest sits on my desk and reminds me that nothing is impossible with God. His provision may come in unexpected ways, but when I listen and obey, His miracle-working power can do great and mighty things through me and others. He can make dreams come true. All it takes is a listening ear to hear the whisper of the Spirit and sharp eyes to catch His movements. The Holy Spirit is ready and able to direct our actions if we pay attention to His leading. Sometimes letting go of our plans and going with the Holy Spirit's flow may seem risky. "Read the gospels and look for Jesus' daily agenda. It just isn't there. Scan the book of Acts to find the apostolic liturgy. You'll come up empty. What you will find are people moving in spontaneous obedience as they are propelled by the fresh wind of the Holy Spirit."[6] Don't I know it!

So how do we cultivate our ability to see and follow the direction of the Holy Spirit? First and most important, we need to belong to God. "Whoever belongs to God hears what God says. The reason you do not hear is that you do not belong to God" (John 8:47).

Second, we need to be willing to listen for the whispers of the Spirit. "Whoever has ears, let them hear what the Spirit says to the churches" (Revelation 2:11). The Holy Spirit may impart a Scripture, thought, idea, or name of a person to help. We need to be alert to hear. We can become more intentional listeners when we are aware of what "noise" we have in our lives that may impair our hearing. We may need to remove ourselves from certain settings or conversations, or limit media, technology, or certain activities for a time. If we're holding onto anger, unforgiveness, or any hurt or sin, it's essential to confess it, release it, and get right with God or others. When we have a clean heart, we can hear.

After we listen, we must also be willing to do something. "Do not merely listen to the word, and so deceive yourselves. Do what it says," James reminds us (James 1:22). Simply put, are we willing to obey? Sometimes the Holy Spirit may ask us to do something outrageous or out of our comfort zone that may require faith, courage, or sacrifice. Others may think we are foolish (like Noah, when God asked him to build an ark, or me, when God asked me to charter a bus). However, when we trust God with all of our heart, He will direct our steps.

Finally, we can learn how God communicates with us and try to confirm what we think we're hearing. Henry Blackaby, the author of *Experiencing God: Knowing and Doing the Will of God*, notes, "God speaks by the Holy Spirit through the Bible, prayer, circumstances and the church to reveal Himself, His purpose and His ways."[7] In the case of the four-poster bed, the Holy Spirit put a recurring thought in my head and a sense of urgency about the bed, which put me in touch with Gloria (prayer and circumstances); then I confirmed this calling by consulting with my husband (the church). Because nothing I was doing went against Scripture, I could go forward. The Holy Spirit's leading was further confirmed by Gloria's response and by all the fruits that followed. In fact, the Holy Spirit is in the business of magnifying our small efforts to follow His lead, as the next story shows.

> *The Holy Spirit may ask us to do something outrageous or out of our comfort zone.*

The Holy Spirit Magnifies Our Efforts

I resisted social networking at first. My fear of expanding my network and adding one more thing to my "to do" list overwhelmed me. However, a still, small voice in my heart whispered, "Step forward." So I did. Friend requests flooded in. One was from Brian, a grade-school friend in the Midwest who used to live down the street from my childhood home. Memories of kickball, bike rides, and playing with my beagle made me smile. I hadn't talked to him in years.

One day I received an urgent message from him asking me to

pray for his young adult son, Michael, who was being deployed to war. Immediately the Holy Spirit revealed several Scriptures to pray for Michael, and I sent them to Brian. I geared up to fight on my knees for a soldier I'd never met. "Lord," I prayed, "Your eyes are on those who fear You, whose hope is in Your unfailing love, to deliver them from death. Lord, You are Michael's help and his shield. May Your unfailing love be with him, even as we put our hope in You."

I always looked forward to Brian's updates about his son. After I received a message about several of Michael's fellow soldiers being injured or killed, I sensed an urgency to beef up prayer support for him. I called my mom and she agreed to pray. *Who else should I ask?* I wondered.

One morning as I strolled into the grocery store for my routine cup of coffee, David, an elderly part-time greeter, welcomed me with a cheery, "Hello!"

Invite him to pray, whispered a voice in my heart.

I told David about Michael and invited him to pray. He enthusiastically agreed to join our prayer platoon. Only then did I discover David was a Korean War veteran and had served as a sergeant and paratrooper. He understood war well.

"How's our solider?" he asked one day during my routine stop. "I was up all night praying for his protection and finally felt peace that he is safe."

Several days had passed since Brian's last update, so I didn't know how he was doing. I soon discovered Michael was on a special mission and was unable to communicate. Our prayer platoon continued to fight spiritual battles. Several more days passed. Finally, I received a message that Michael was safe. A few weeks later, Brian posted, "My boy is back!"

After Michael returned home, Brian sent me the following message:

Kathe,

My son told me of a really strange thing that happened to him in Afghanistan. He was up against a wall. The enemy shot all around his body and head. He told me, "I was not afraid at all." The most peaceful feeling came to him, and the most relaxed feeling he'd ever felt. I told him, "God was telling you He was not quite done with you yet."

I joyfully shared this answered prayer with my mom and David. Our prayer platoon rejoiced.

I marvel at God's creativity in working through social networking, two childhood friends, an elderly mother, and a war veteran to help a soldier at war. Prayer is a powerful weapon that knows no geographical boundaries or time zones. Through prayer, we tap into the enormous power of the Spirit, who is able to magnify our smallest efforts to spread hope around the world.

> *Through prayer, we tap into the enormous power of the Spirit.*

Because I can't help but rejoice in the power of the Spirit, I have to share one final story that illustrates God's ability to do immeasurably more than we can imagine.

Immeasurably More

When my husband, Rich, was eight, his dad died. Rich found some comfort in knowing the Christian grade school that he attended in St. Louis, Missouri, was started by his dad. Perhaps that's why my husband was so quick to say yes to our pastor's invitation to chair a committee to determine if our church should start a Christian school in Arizona. The thought of following in his dad's footsteps to create a legacy for his sons energized him.

My husband recalls weeks of research, meetings, and hours of fervent prayer seeking God's will. "Finally, I sensed God wanted us to step out in faith, so I stood before the elders and encouraged them to start the school," Rich said.

In 1995, Bethany Christian School started in Arizona with twenty-two students, one teacher, and my husband and a few others serving on the school board. My job was to pray in a van with another mom, which later spread to a gathering of several moms and our first Moms in Touch group (now Moms in Prayer), which continues to this day at the school. Through the years we witnessed many challenges and miracles, including the school becoming independent from the church, and a major fundraising campaign that entailed buying and remodeling a shopping center to house our school. Faith and prayer were the guiding principles of the school and continue to this day.

One year the school's theme verse was: "Now to Him who is able to do immeasurably more than all we ask or imagine, according to His power that is at work within us" (Ephesians 3:20).

When my friend Lisa Kowalski suggested we order and distribute tape-measure bracelets to support our school's "Immeasurably More" campaign, I had no conception how this idea would spread. The multicolored bracelets were made by a woman from another state from a two-sided measuring tape and included adjustable snaps. Every time I wore a bracelet, random people would ask about it. When they did, I'd share the bracelet's theme verse, Ephesians 3:20, then slip it off, hand it to them, and say, "It will remind you that God is immeasurably more; He is bigger than anything you face."

Over the months that followed, long after the school campaign had ended, I ordered more bracelets. My "immeasurably more bracelet" became part of my daily attire. When I wore it, I expected people to ask me about it—and they did. I handed out dozens of them to people who asked about it: grocery store clerks, doctors, baristas, executives on airplanes, and women waiting for their mammogram. When several people approached me to buy them as gifts, I sensed God enlarging their purpose not only for hope to hand out, but also to fund hurting women on my bus trips. I prayed and sensed the Holy Spirit leading me forward.

One day, I went to get my hair colored at the beauty college. Not only did the low cost appeal to me, but the stylists-in-training setting is a great place to spread hope. I followed my new stylist to her chair. Within a few minutes we were chatting, and I discovered she was from Minnesota. When she asked about my bracelet, I shared the verse, slipped it off, and handed it to her as a gift.

"My mom could really use this," she said.

Then we brainstormed ways she could encourage her mom.

A few days later, I received this email:

Hi, Kathe,

My daughter Chloe is in school at the Institute in Arizona and shared the story of the bracelet. She also told me how much she loves and values talking to you. I'm seventeen hundred miles away, so I don't get to see her often, and my best source of comfort is in keeping her in my prayers each day. Your presence in her life at just the right time is one of the blessings that clearly is an answer to my prayers. What a simple, but profound way in which you've had a loving impact on her life! Thank you!

I was greeted at church this morning with several requests for your "immeasurably more" bracelets. You have struck a chord with these and the folks up here in Fridley, Minnesota. Are these available?

Thanks,
Matt

When I read Matt's letter, I knew the Holy Spirit was confirming my decision about the bracelets as a source for funding women on bus trips. So I mailed two dozen bracelets to my stylist's dad in Minnesota to hand out hope, and the money I received from him helped me spread more hope. You never know how God will use a word, a listening ear, or an ordinary object like a bracelet to make a difference. When you give hope away, it spreads. Truly, the Spirit is able to do immeasurably more than we can ask or imagine.

> When you give hope away, it spreads.

The next time you hear "pop, pop, pop" in a microwave, ask, "Am I relying on the Holy Spirit's power or on my own strength?" When you feel anxious or defeated, throw up your hands as an act of surrender or praise. Only the Holy Spirit can give us the power we need to become the hopelifters He intends for us to be. Not even this book and all the creative ideas inside it can truly give lasting hope to hurting people — nothing but God can. Our part is to listen and respond when He calls, staying alert to His whispers in our hearts, watching for His movement in our circumstances, and confirming His call through prayer, Scripture, and other trusted believers. Will you join me in tapping into the wonder-working power of the Holy Spirit, then rejoice with me as we celebrate His ability to magnify our smallest efforts?

CHAPTER 5

HOPE
IN A PLACE

My people will live in peaceful dwelling places,
in secure homes, in undisturbed places of rest.
—ISAIAH 32:18

"Offer your extra bedroom to someone who is hurting!"

Brenda Dull knew this repeated thought had to be from God. But the bedroom was in no condition to host anyone. Her roommate had moved out, leaving the room trashed. The walls were marked with holes, and the carpet was filthy, stained, and worn. Brenda had limited funds from severe health challenges that forced her to close her business, and she didn't have the strength or resources to undertake the renovations on her own. So she prayed and asked God to provide help to refurbish the room. Amazingly, a group at her church heard about her dream and adopted her spare bedroom. They painted, installed a new floor, and provided new fixtures, furniture, and decorative items.

"God, use this room to transform hurting hearts into hope-filled ones," Brenda prayed.

Within a short time, the Lord connected Brenda to women in need of hope, and she offered them her room. Some (like me) came for an afternoon retreat, while others in deep crisis stayed longer. Her extra room became a refuge of hope for hurting women. Brenda's part was to pray, provide simple refreshments, and offer her presence as needed. Brenda's growing guest book of names is a reminder of how God can use a place to make a difference. And her ministry is a reminder that hope can be found in a *place*.

Hope in a Home

Home is a word that implies safety, comfort, and love. When we are at home, we can relax and be ourselves. Home is where we meet with loved ones, where we are nourished with good food, where we rest after a long day of work or school. None of us can feel hope unless we can feel a deep sense of being "at home."

The Bible quietly points out this important need. In his public ministry, Jesus wandered from place to place, but He found rest in the homes of those who loved Him. Martha was one of those people who "opened her home to Him" (Luke 10:38).

"Home" is also an important theme of the book of Ruth. When Naomi's husband died, she decided to return "home" to Judah, and encouraged her daughters-in-law, also widows, to stay in their "home" of Moab. But to Ruth, home was not to be found in either Judah or Moab, but in the person of Naomi

> *None of us can feel hope unless we can feel a deep sense of being "at home."*

herself and the God she worshiped. When Naomi urged Ruth to go back to Moab, Ruth refused, declaring, "Where you go I will go, and where you stay I will stay. Your people will be my people and your God my God" (Ruth 1:16). True, Ruth eventually found a new home in Bethlehem and a new husband in Boaz. But for her, "home" started with her relationship with Naomi and her faith in Naomi's God. When Naomi allowed Ruth to come home to Judah with her, she shared more than a place. She shared her heart.

Like Ruth, Erica Carlson found hope in a relative's home and heart. Her husband was deployed for a year, and as a young wife with no children, Erica was feeling overwhelmed with loneliness. The house seemed so big. She was feeling alone and was quickly becoming hopeless.

At Thanksgiving dinner, Erica connected with one of her husband's aunts and realized they were kindred spirits. Aunt Bonnie invited Erica for a weekend getaway at her home three hours away. Lonely and sad, Erica eagerly took the opportunity for a change of scenery. During her stay, Erica kept her hands busy, working on projects with Aunt Bonnie. They talked and got to know one another, which kept Erica's mind busy, and they simply enjoyed being together. They went to a play put on by a local school, went to church, and played board games with Bonnie's husband, Ron.

Nothing they did was extraordinary, but Erica had found a friend and a home in Aunt Bonnie. Erica had productive activities to keep her hands, mind, and heart busy, and she had fewer opportunities to sit around and think about her husband being at war. They both enjoyed the visit so much that Aunt Bonnie invited her back to her home again, and it soon became a regular event. Erica savored the time spent with Aunt Bonnie and looked forward to the next project they would do or the next game played. During a lonely time in her life, Aunt Bonnie's friendship was a comfort and a hope. Aunt Bonnie offered Erica a place not only in her home, but also in her heart.

Hope at a River

Hope is not only found at home. Other places, even nature, can inspire or encourage you, still your soul, or connect you with God. Jesus found hope in early mornings in the wilderness (Mark 1:35). Moses met with God on Mount Sinai (Exodus 24:13). Hannah trekked annually to Shiloh to pray (1 Samuel 1:1–18).

I find hope at the river. The sound of rushing water refreshes me and reminds me of childhood days wading barefoot through Castor River in rural Marquand, Missouri, catching tadpoles and roasting hotdogs along the river bank. When I married and moved to Eugene, Oregon, I was fortunate to work near the Willamette River, another inspiring setting.

Then we were abruptly transferred to Phoenix, Arizona. An ocean of sand was the norm where I lived. When my friend Brenda Dull suggested I go to Living Water Retreat Center for a personal retreat, my parched soul perked up. I made a reservation and drove there a few days later. When I arrived at the lush, serene setting, I thought I was back in the Midwest. A horse trotted in a field near the tree-lined pond. I strolled through the field by a pathway of benches. Then I heard a familiar sound. Rushing water! A few steps later, I gazed into Oak Creek's rippling blue-green water and immediately felt renewed and revived. I've been going there ever since.

What setting or place inspires you? Even if you can't get to the place your heart desires, could your creativity get you there? When I yearn for a river and can't get to one, I go sit in my hall bathroom, turn on the faucet, and look at the mural of Castor River painted on my bathroom wall.

One day, I overhead a grieving coworker who had lost her mother say, "I wish I could go to the beach." My creativity started churning. The next morning, I arrived early and left a gift on her desk: a sand bucket filled with a beach towel, sunglasses, flip flops, her favorite soft drink, and a sounds of the ocean CD. The anonymous card said, "Enjoy the beach tonight!"

Heaven Is a Place

Ultimately, our longing for a place of love, security, and rest is a heart cry for our final home: heaven. Heaven is a real place where all believers in Jesus Christ will live for eternity. It's a bright, glorious place with streets of gold, a variety of fruit-bearing trees, houses with many rooms, and a crystal-clear river flowing from the throne of God (see John 14:2 and Revelation 22:1–5). Best of all, God himself will be there.

The apostle John had a glorious vision of heaven: "I saw the Holy City, the new Jerusalem, coming down out of heaven from God, prepared as a bride beautifully dressed for her husband. And I heard a loud voice from the throne saying, 'Look! God's dwelling is now among the people, and He will dwell with them. They will be His people, and God Himself will be with them and be their God. He will wipe every tear from their eyes. There will be no more death or mourning or crying or pain, for the old order of things has passed away'" (Revelation 21:2–5).

I've read many Scriptures about heaven and tried to imagine what my future home will be like.[8] In his book *Heaven*, Randy Alcorn paints a picture for us:

> Our first glimpse of heaven will cause us to gasp in amazement and delight. The first gasp will likely be followed by many more as we continually encounter new sights in that endlessly wonderful place. Imagine it—all of it—in original condition. The happy dog with the wagging tail, not the snarling beast, beaten and starved. The flower unwilted, the grass undying, the blue sky without pollution. People smiling and joyful, not angry, depressed and empty. Think of friends and family members who loved Jesus and are with him now. Picture them with you, walking together in this place. All of you have powerful bodies ... Now you see someone coming toward you. It's Jesus with a big smile on His face. You fall to your knees to worship. He pulls you up and embraces you. At last you're with the person you were made for, in a place you were meant to be.[9]

I can hardly wait to experience this amazing place. Sometimes I get homesick for heaven, and like Paul I'm torn between my life here on earth and my longing for my eternal home with Jesus in heaven (see Philippians 1:23). So many friends and loved ones reside there, including my son John Samuel, who died shortly after birth, and my other three unborn babies. I look forward to seeing them again. What a reunion that will be!

Hope is a place, and its name is heaven, our ultimate place of love, security, and rest.

Unfortunately, multitudes in our world have not accepted Jesus Christ and are hurting spiritually. Their eternal home will be a horrible place called hell, where they will be separated from God and those of us who love him, forever. Second Thessalonians 1:8–9 warns, "[God] will punish those who do not know God and do not obey the gospel of our Lord Jesus. They will be punished with everlasting destruction and shut out from the presence of the Lord and from the glory of His might."

Spreading eternal hope to the world is urgent. Telling unbelievers about Jesus and inviting them to know they have a place for all eternity in heaven is a daily opportunity we must embrace. Remind them that hope is a place, and its name is heaven, our ultimate place of love, security, and rest.

CHAPTER 6

HOPE
IN A PROCESS

. . . we also rejoice in our sufferings, because we know that suffering produces perseverance; perseverance, character; and character, hope. And hope does not disappoint us.
—ROMANS 5:3–5a (NIV 1984)

An oversized pair of turquoise sunglasses sits on my desk. When I wear them I usually get a laugh from my clown-like appearance, yet they also represent my creative, hopeful side that loves to envision the God-given potential of anyone or anything. Seeing beyond what is to what could be energizes me. God's reality isn't always how it appears to human eyes, and circumstances often cloud our vision. Could obstacles really be viewed as opportunities in disguise? Are hopeless situations really miracles in the making? Is gut-wrenching pain and suffering a pathway for God's power and hope to be unleashed? My big glasses remind me to look up and invite God to enlarge my vision and my heart to be His hope to a hurting world. They also remind me to look beyond any circumstance and see hope in a process.

> God's reality isn't always how it appears to human eyes

S + P + C = H

"Hope is found in a process," I announced to my class, then pointed to the following equation on the board: S + P + C = H.

A sea of questioning eyes stared back at me. So I opened my Bible to Romans 5:3–4 and began to explain, "We rejoice in our suffering (S), because suffering produces perseverance (P), perseverance produces character (C), and character produces hope (H)."

Nodding heads confirmed the women understood the equation and agreed. I knew many of their personal stories: struggles with addiction, prodigal children, divorce, loss, unemployment, bankruptcy, and illness. As I looked around the room, I realized *everyone* was somewhere in the process of hope. Some women were suffering (S) deeply from a recent crisis or life circumstance. Others were several months along in their persevering (P) journey. Several had experienced deep changes in their character (C), becoming more patient, more forgiving, more courageous. A few reflected a supernatural peace and confidence—a deep and abiding hope (H)—and overflowed with compassion to comfort others.

The truth is, wherever you are in the process, you have hope. Even if your suffering feels ugly and unbearable, remember, you have hope. As you persevere, you have hope. As your character develops, never forget, you have hope. Regardless of your circumstance, you can rest in your relationship with God, knowing that He is in the process with you. He is your hope.

$$S + P + C = H$$

Where are you in the process of hope today?

Divine Possibilities

When God looks at a hurting person or at a hopeless circumstance, anything is possible. He always sees beyond human comprehension. He looked beyond an elderly father and a barren womb to Abraham and Sarah, the father and mother of nations. He saw beyond Joseph's betrayal and his imprisonment to Joseph saving starving nations. When God gazed at captive Israelites, He saw them delivered and living in the Promised Land. Beyond a baby in the manger, He saw a Savior for a hurting world. When He saw a desperate bleeding woman, He saw her healed by a touch of Jesus' robe. When God looked at a few loaves and fishes, He didn't give up; He saw thousands of hungry people fed. God looked beyond the cross and an empty tomb, to eternal hope for His people.

When the doctor announced, "Your baby is going to die!" I entered into my season of suffering (S). Perhaps you've read my story in one of my books, *Grieving the Loss of a Loved One* or *Grieving the Child I Never Knew.* If you haven't, here's the condensed version. After years of infertility, losing a child through miscarriage, and adopting a baby, I discovered at age thirty-seven I was pregnant. However, my short-lived joy turned to sorrow on Good Friday when my fourteen-week ultrasound revealed our unborn son was anen-cephalic (a neuro-tube defect where the brain and skull do not form properly and the prognosis is death).

That Easter weekend I experienced my personal Gethsemane and cried out to God to remove my cup of suffering (S). By Easter morn-ing, I made a decision to surrender my will to God's and asked for his strength to endure my journey (P). God had prepared me to carry this cross and had even provided a journey with a friend a decade earlier with the same rare diagnosis.

During the next twenty-eight weeks, God poured out his love for me through people who handed out hope to me in ordinary and extraordinary ways. He enabled me to persevere (P). And on August 22, 1996, John Samuel was born looking up at God, and within a few hours he was ushered into heaven.

John Samuel's brief life initiated a sea of change in my character (C). I used to be a person who rarely cried, who could be abrupt and say, "Get over it." However, the Holy Spirit's power at work in and through me has transformed me into a different person with a compassionate heart. My eyes began to be opened to the hurts of those around me.

When I was asked to write my books *Grieving the Loss of a Loved One* and *Grieving the Child I Never Knew,* my first thought was, *Are you crazy?* Fortunately, I prayed about it before responding and asked God to show me His plan for my writing. I began to picture faces of grieving people I knew and realized this was an opportunity for me to encourage them and others who were grieving, because I under-stood the language of loss. My life experience could point others to my powerful, comforting God, who would help them, too. Years and thousands of readers later, I know I made the right choice to share my life experience with others, bringing hope (H) not only to them, but to my own grieving heart. Thank God that he showed me the divine possibilities that were present in my experience of suffering.

What is your experience of suffering? How have you persevered through it? How has it built your character? Are you at a point now where you can find hope in your suffering, and in turn can offer that hope to others in need? Wherever you are in the equation of S + P + C = H, remember, you *are* in the hope process. Try not to hurry the progression; rather, embrace where you are and recognize a divine work is being done in you. And hope is the result of that process.

Kim's Story

When Kim Slaughter discovered she was pregnant, it was one of the happiest days of her life. An ultrasound confirmed, "It's a girl." Kim dreamed of frilly dresses and tying bows in her daughter's hair. Then, just three weeks before Kim's due date, her doctor's words shattered her motherhood dream: "Your baby has no heartbeat."

In shock and disbelief, Kim plummeted to the depths of suffering. She would have to face the unthinkable: to birth a child who would never breathe. How would she endure this? She cried out to God for help. A supernatural peace and confidence flowed through her and helped her persevere. On November 9, Narissa Ashley Slaughter, Kim's stillborn daughter, was born. Although Kim didn't understand why God allowed her loss, she knew God had a plan, and she trusted Him to bring hope in the process of her suffering.

Over time, Kim's heart of compassion grew. She started a support group for grieving mothers suffering the loss of a child. Making a memory quilt, designing a scrapbook page, and hosting a child dedication program are a few of the creative ways Kim brings hope to suffering women. Now other churches are asking Kim to help them start groups to spread hope too.

Kim's loss (S) led her to cry out to God, who helped her persevere

(P), and he developed compassion in her character (C), so she would start a support group to help others (H).

Hope is always in process, and sometimes it may surprise us how it comes full circle. The book born out of my suffering— *Grieving the Child I Never Knew*—helped Kim persevere through her grief, and now she uses it in her support groups for other grieving mothers. When we open our lives to God's work, He enlarges our vision to include divine possibilities, and hope is born and spread.

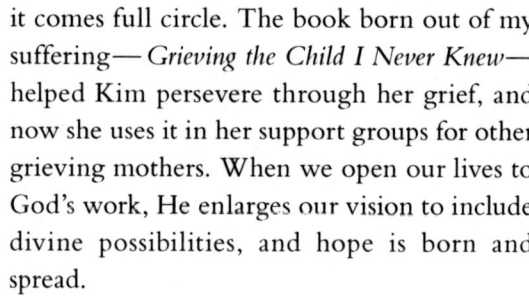

Hope is always in process; it may surprise us how it comes full circle.

Our creative Creator can do immeasurably more than we think or imagine according to His power at work within us. He invites us to join Him in His work to help a hurting world. Together, let's look through the lenses of God-sized potential and see hope in fresh ways. There are unlimited possibilities to help others. It's up to us to find them and use them.

CHAPTER 7

HOPE IN
A POSSESSION

*All the believers were one in heart and mind. No one claimed
that any of their possessions was their own, but they shared
everything they had . . . there were no needy persons among
them.*

—ACTS 4:32, 34

I grew up in a small town in a family of small business owners and
relatives who served others. Grandpa owned the general store. Dad
owned the gas station. Mom owned the beauty shop (hair salon).
Uncle June was the postmaster, and Aunt Wilma worked at the bank.
We even had a gospel quartet of singing cousins who performed.
Occasionally, they sang for Uncle Bob at a funeral. He was the
undertaker. As a child, I played hide and seek around his empty cas-
kets. Little did I know then that even this unique experience would
help prepare me to become a hopelifter and serve hurting people.

When someone died in our community, our family banded
together, each one doing his or her part to serve the needs of the
grieving family. We provided practical things like food, clothing,
flowers, tissues, a casket, money, and gas for cars. We also offered
services and talents like funeral planning, hair styling, and singing.
By working together to share our resources, our family met needs in
the community and brought hope to people in need, even through
a funeral.

The church is also a community with its variety of gifts that can
meet needs. The Bible tells us that the early church of believers lived
in caring, unified community with one another, sharing everything

they had (Acts 4:32). I've tried to imagine what it would feel like to live in a one-heart, one-mind community with all physical and spiritual possessions pooled together and available for use.

If I needed transportation, I could go to the resource bank and choose from a Corvette, van, motorcycle, or skateboard offered by my neighbors. If I got hungry, I could enlist people with cooking talents and savor the meal they'd prepare — of course, the helpers in the group would show up and do the dishes. Likewise, when someone needed prayer or encouragement through a life loss, I'd do my part. When the believers in the early church shared their possessions, there were no needy persons among them (Acts 4:34). As Bible stories often show, God can use a possession we share with others to address a need and proclaim his power.

> *When the believers shared their possessions, there were no needy persons among them.*

By divine direction, a penniless widow opened her home for Elijah to stay. All she had left to eat was a handful of flour and a little oil. When he asked her for bread, she shared her burdened heart with him — she was about to prepare her last meal for her and her son, and then they would die. Elijah listened, then he gave her hope. He promised that her near-empty jug of oil and flour would not run out if she fed him. This was a real test of self-denial and faith for her. What would happen if she gave her last bit of food away? Would she starve? Her faith was rewarded when she shared what she had. God multiplied her possessions, her flour and oil never ran out, and she, Elijah, and her son were fed daily (1 Kings 17:7 – 16).

When Jesus asked the disciples to feed the hungry crowd, Andrew found a young boy with a few loaves and fish, who offered them to Jesus. I wonder if Andrew (or the little boy who offered them) had any idea what his sharing would yield that day. Thousands were fed and many baskets of leftovers remained as a tangible reminder of God's miracle-working power (John 6:4 – 14). This story encourages us that God will use our possessions to address needs. Not only that,

He will even *multiply* what we give, if we are faithful to do our part and offer what we have.

In our journey to be a hopelifter, we have endless opportunities to offer our resources and possessions to spread hope. Yet sometimes we miss them because we don't fully understand what possessions

> *God can transform anything we offer Him to bring hope to someone in need.*
>

we have to offer or we minimize their value. God can transform *anything* we offer Him, big or small, old or new, even forgotten items, to bring hope to someone in need, when we listen, obey, and release it to Him.

Offering Our Possessions

One Friday morning during my toddler's morning nap, the doorbell rang. I could hardly wait to open the door and usher my friend inside. Her weekly visit to clean my home and listen to me pour out my heart was the highlight of my week. Motherhood in my forties to a teenager and a toddler was harder than I expected. I struggled to keep my life, work, and home in order. I desperately needed acts of service, and a group of my friends knew it. So they surprised me for my fortieth birthday and paid for several weeks of housecleaning.

After sharing laughter, conversation, and a cup of coffee together, we decided we'd better get to work before my young son woke up. I had proclaimed Fridays my personal "get 'er done" day when I would complete any undone projects I didn't enjoy doing. Somehow, having my friend in the home motivated me and propelled me forward. As I went upstairs to get started, a thought popped into my mind: *Give her your purple nightgown.*

Purple nightgown? I didn't have a purple nightgown, and even if I did, I wouldn't give my friend something so personal, especially if it was used.

Give her your purple nightgown.

The second time this thought came, I stopped and prayed. *Show me what you mean.*

I went into my closet and stood there. Then I remembered the stack of maternity clothes I had in the corner. As I sorted through them, I saw it at the bottom of the stack ... a purple nightgown.

I'd only worn it a few times and had purchased it because it made me feel attractive during my last few weeks of pregnancy. Nightgowns are personal, and I'm not sure I would be open to wearing another woman's. Offering my purple nightgown to a new friend could be awkward, and I didn't want to offend her. Still, as I prayed, I sensed I should offer her the nightgown.

Unexpectedly, she walked into my room, so I knew this was the right moment.

"Would you like this purple nightgown?" I asked.

She looked surprised, then she started to laugh. I learned that purple was her favorite color and that she had prayed earlier that week for a romantic evening with her husband and to feel special and loved. Someone had given her a gift certificate and now—a purple nightgown!

Physical possessions, even personal and used ones, may bring timely hope to someone in need. Declare a cleaning day. Enlist a friend to join you in cleaning out a closet or spare room to search for unused or forgotten treasures. Pray and ask God to search not only your home, but your heart for the hidden reason you are unwilling to let go of possessions you have. Ask Him to help you become a better steward of what has been entrusted to you. One woman I know has a personal rule that when she purchases a new item, she must get rid of an old one.

Needy people are everywhere. They may not all be starving or homeless, but an everyday friend who may silently desires something you may have, could bring her hope. Invite Jesus to give you a willing, selfless heart to share your possessions with others. When you offer what you have to Him, expect Him to multiply hope. And if He tells you to offer a possession to someone ... trust Him, and give.

Offering Our Skills and Talents

Skills and talents are also valuable possessions that we can offer to bring hope to hurting people. As we saw in my previous story, cleaning was a skill my friend offered to me, and that encouraged me in a season of great need. *A skill* is a learned ability while a *talent* is an effortless, natural ability. For example, my mom never took a music lesson in her life but was a talented musician. She possessed a natural ability to play the piano. Both skills and talents can be employed to bring hope.

Skills can often be divided into general and specific skills. For example, in the area of work, general skills would include time management, teamwork, leadership, and motivation. You may also possess a more specific skill in one or more of the following areas: work, life, people, or social. For example, teaching children is a work skill. Organizing or cleaning a home is a life skill. Listening and perceiving needs is a people skill, and communicating easily to others is a social skill. In our community, church, and home, we need a variety of skills to function. Even a simple social skill of saying "hello" to a stranger can make a difference in someone's life.

One morning I stopped for coffee and noticed the woman next to me looked stressed (social skill). When I asked, "How are you today?" she burst into tears. Over the next hour I listened (people skill) to her share her painful experience of dealing with the divorce she didn't want, being a single mom to two teenage girls, struggling with health challenges, and trying to find work. Although I couldn't solve all of her problems, listening was a gift I could give in that moment. Then I asked her, "What is the one thing in your life that is stressing you out the most today?"

She immediately replied, "My kitchen! There are piles of stuff everywhere."

"Would you be willing to allow me and a few friends to organize your kitchen this Friday?" I asked.

She nodded in disbelief and started to cry again, but this time tears of relief. A few days later, I showed up with three "organizing" friends (the kind who love to alphabetize spices), and we spent the day transforming her kitchen into a purposeful, tidy, hopeful place (life skill). Never underestimate the power of using your skills and talents to bring hope to people.

What skills and talents do you have that could help others?

Offering Our Life Experiences

We also possess valuable insights, information, and lessons learned from what we have experienced through our personal lives. I believe we go through what we go through, to help others go through what we went through. Life experiences are unique and priceless possessions that can offer hope to someone else going through a similar life stage or challenge.

For example, when I felt called to create and grow a ministry to professional women, I prayed for someone who had "been there, experienced that," and could provide a life résumé or "experiential" resources about how to lead, find volunteers, develop a board, and fundraise.

One day, I was so discouraged by the growing tension within my board, I was considering stepping down. Although it was an exciting season of ministry and growing numbers of women were being encouraged in the workplace, I felt as if my vision was being squelched. So I prayed and asked God to connect me to someone who could relate to my life experience and give me insights. Pastor Tucker's name came to mind. He'd been my pastor for several years, and after resigning from our church, he now worked as a consultant and interim pastor to churches in transition. Pastor Tucker understood the private pain leaders endure with their boards. I believed his personal experience, successes, and mistakes could help me at this pivotal time in my leadership journey.

Sure enough, when we met he listened, asked questions, and shared. He affirmed my vision and encouraged my leadership heart. He helped me develop new strategies to use my people and social skills with board members whose personality and communication style differed from mine. I'll never forget his simple advice he'd learned from his own life experience: "Keep your friends close and your enemies closer." Pastor Tucker's timely words and his willingness to share his life experience that day helped me persevere in that leadership role for a few more years.

Start thinking about your life experiences, good or bad, as a possession you could offer to someone, and bring them hope like Pastor Tucker did for me.

Offering Our Spiritual Gifts

God provides a variety of resources to help us grow, mature, and serve as believers. For example, the Holy Spirit, the Bible, and the church are available spiritual resources to us.

Spiritual gifts are another resource we need to discover or review so we can serve others beyond our human limitations of physical possessions, skills, talents, and experiences. Don't skip this part even if you think you know what it is; you might be surprised at a fresh revelation. Or you might be encouraged to dig deeper and evaluate your gifts to discover if a new gift has emerged for this season of your life.

The first place in the New Testament you find the term "spiritual gift" is Romans 1:11-12. Paul says, "I long to see you so that I may impart to you some spiritual gift to make you strong—that is, that you and I may be mutually encouraged by each other's faith." We learn from this verse that spiritual gifts are for *strengthening* others. God doesn't want us to hoard them.

Spiritual gifts are for strengthening others.

How do we get spiritual gifts? So many people seem to be confused about this. In 1 Corinthians 12, we learn that spiritual gifts are given to God's people by the Holy Spirit for "the common good." Verse 11 says the gifts are given according to God's sovereign will ("as He determines"). Ephesians 4:12 tells us these gifts are given to prepare God's people for service and for building up the body of Christ. God decides what spiritual gifts a believer is entrusted with to use for His glory.

In 1991, my husband and I attended an inductive Bible study

about spiritual gifts through Precept Ministries International. The ministry, founded by Kay Arthur, teaches people how to study God's Word. Although the Lord had already shown me how to study His Word, He used this study to confirm that I was on the right track, and to ignite my passion to know and discover my gift(s) and learn how to use them effectively.

The study pointed us to key passages about spiritual gifts in Romans 12; 1 Corinthians 12; 14; Ephesians 4; and 1 Peter 4. It also reminded us that God's Word is the authority and we must be careful to not mishandle it by taking words out of context.

I discovered one of my spiritual gifts at that season was exhortation —giving encouragement to others. As I exercised my gift, I reached out to encourage the leader of our group, and she and I became friends and coworkers for the kingdom.

A few years later, I hungered to know more about my purpose and gifts, so I attended a small group, called SoulWork, led by my friend and mentor Holly DelHousaye. Our band of a few women committed to meet regularly for a year to help one another grow and discover our purpose. One week after answering several questions about my spiritual gifts, I was surprised that more gifts had emerged. As I processed this new information with Holly and the group, I learned that God may have used many of my life experiences of suffering to shape my newly discovered spiritual gifts of mercy and faith. Fortunately, others in my group had gifts of wisdom and knowledge, which I needed at the time, to help me complete a crucial assignment.

Offering All You Have and Are

"Two words."

That was Holly's directive—to write a personal mission statement using only two words. This task seemed impossible for my chatty-Kathe style, but I vowed I would finish the assignment. Throughout the week, I prayed, reviewed the page of words Holly gave us, and reviewed my spiritual gifts. I began to "try on" words to see if they fit me. Finally, I found the right fit (or so I thought) and bounded into our group ready to be affirmed. When it was my turn, I belted out, "Encourage potential!"

I waited. A few of the women nodded their heads, but I noticed my friend Mary Jane looked perplexed. Finally, she spoke, "That's not big enough for you!"

I knew her spiritual gift of wisdom was being used. She also knew me well through our many years of friendship and the life experiences we had encountered together. So, I listened and told the group I would continue praying for God to reveal His two bigger words to me. The night before class, He finally answered when I spotted an oversized pair of glasses in the store. Two words popped into my head: *Envision potential.*

That's it! I thought.

When I walked into the room the next day sporting my new glasses and presented my words, the group erupted with cheers and applause.

> *Jesus will multiply hope beyond what you ever imagined.*

Hope *can* be found in a possession when we offer it in Jesus' name. As you consider your possessions, remember to pray first, and then ask God, the giver of all possessions, to reveal what you have to offer—your physical possessions, skills, talents, life experiences, and spiritual gifts—to share with others who may need what you have. You may discover something new you didn't know you had or find a hidden treasure long forgotten. Your part in the body of Christ is unique and needed to build others up. When you offer all you have and are to Jesus and trust Him, He will multiply hope beyond what you ever imagined. Envision *His* potential.

CHAPTER 8

HOPE IN
A CONNECTION

*Now you are the body of Christ, and each one of you is a
part of it. . . . If one part suffers, every part suffers with it;
if one part is honored, every part rejoices with it.*
—1 CORINTHIANS 12:27, 26

One day, my friend Debbie Mis and I were on a trip to spend time
as friends, and we made an unexpected stop for a restroom break. On
our way back to the car, I felt prompted to talk to an older woman
and her friend. I discovered these two friends were on a sightseeing
trip from Michigan. To my surprise, I learned she lived in Grand
Rapids, Michigan, where I would be traveling later that year for a
conference. What amazed me more was finding out she was a Christian, lived directly across the street from the campus where our conference would be held, and frequently housed guests. We exchanged
contact information and started emailing one another. I invited her
to come as my guest to the Speak Up Conference, and to my surprise
and delight, she came. I introduced her as "Pit Stop Pat," and she
became a regular supporter of the annual conference.

The next year, Pat opened her home to conference attendees who
couldn't afford the cost of a hotel, and the year after that she enlisted
her neighbor to house people too. Pat usually attended my Hopelifter
workshop and enjoyed when I told people our story of how God
connected us. Besides housing conference attendees, she was passionate about helping those leaving prison to transition successfully.
Her desire to help anyone in need was obvious during one of my
workshops. A man with a speech impediment and other challenges

attended and shared his desire to be an encourager. Pat listened intently, then spoke up to encourage him with a list of resources.

Although Pat is now at a rest stop in heaven, I'm grateful to God for helping me find hope through her. She is one of many miraculous connections that God has orchestrated, joining me to someone I need, someone who needs me, or best of all, someone I need who also needs me!

The Body of Christ

The early church gives us a glimpse of the heavenly power of connection. On the cross, knowing His grieving mother, Mary, would need a supportive presence after He died, Jesus entrusted her to His beloved disciple, John. I'm sure He knew that her deeply reflective spirit would find a home in the heart of His most sensitive of disciples. (Peter may have had his strong points, but he probably wasn't the most perceptive or gentle person.)

God planned a way to connect Saul—the persecutor of his people—and Ananias, a faithful disciple who was shocked at God's command to restore Saul's vision and make him a leader of the infant church (Acts 9:10–18). When Saul was lonely and needed a friend because the disciples "were all afraid of him, not believing that he really was a disciple" (9:26), Barnabas "brought him to the apostles" (9:27) and told them how Jesus had spoken to Saul (later called Paul). God chose a couple, Priscilla and Aquila, to encourage Paul by having him live with them (Acts 18:3). Paul invited Timothy, a younger companion and "true son in the faith" (1 Timothy 1:2), to join his missionary team, and within a few years he became Paul's traveling troubleshooter to the churches.

By God's design we are interconnected.

The church, the body of Christ, is like a human body made up of many parts. Each part is different, yet every part is needed to contribute to a healthy, whole body. By God's design, we are interconnected. "If one part suffers, every part suffers with it; if one part is honored, every part rejoices with it" (1 Corinthians 12:26).

Paul understood this well, and he experienced hope in the connections God orchestrated in his life. Each person played a unique role in bringing hope to his life by using their gift and doing their part.

Which part are you in the body of Christ? Are you a bold, proclaiming prophet like Paul? Or is your part to serve or connect others to timely resources like Pit Stop Pat? Do you enjoy encouraging others like Barnabas, or is your part to provide your hospitality, like Priscilla and Aquila? Every part is vital in the body of Christ. Whatever part and gift you represent, use it. Be alert and ready to respond when God links you to another person. Invite God to show you how you can use your gifts to glorify Him and bring others hope.

> *Be alert and ready to respond when God links you to another person.*

God may go to extreme measures to connect you to someone who is hurting. His divine connections are limitless and powerful. As you'll see in the following story, don't be surprised if His hope spreads in ways you never imagined.

The Power of Connection

The publication of *Grieving the Loss of a Loved One* and *Grieving the Child I Never Knew* opened many doors for me to speak and share my story with groups all over the country. When I met Heather White in Dallas, I was speaking at a convention. After my workshop, she invited me to ride to Starbucks in a red Corvette, and I enthusiastically agreed. I discovered we shared a common bond: we had both lost a child. She told me she flew to Dallas in hopes of meeting me after reading my book. Amazingly, I discovered she lived in Arizona, not far from me. Meeting Heather White was the first of a series of miraculous connections that God orchestrated to bring hope and healing into a web of lives.

A few weeks later, Heather and I met again, this time at an Arizona Starbucks. Heather brought along a hurting friend, Gia Chapman. I listened to Gia share her story of losing her infant daughter,

Sable Marie, from a rare disorder. Little did I know then how God would spread hope through our broken hearts and build a partnership between Gia and me to help other grieving moms. Over the next few years, the three of us continued to meet for coffee, and we celebrated pregnancies, an adopted baby, and Gia's new ministry, Sable's Wings, supporting grieving families who lost a child.

One day over coffee, I told Gia—who had been on my first bus trip—of my dream to have a Mother's Day bus trip for women who had lost children. Gia immediately left the table, then returned a few minutes later and plopped a check on the table. "Sable's Wings wants to help!" she said.

I was shocked and overwhelmed by this unexpected gift to provide the cost of transportation for grieving moms. Although I was the one who originally encouraged Gia, she then turned around and encouraged me—an example of God's creative power of hope in connection.

Hope Spreads

Not only does hope connect us to each other, but it is also contagious —in other words, the connections keep spreading! Here's an example from my own life when a web of interconnected lives spread hope and healing as far as my eyes could see—and beyond!

When I read Shayla Van Hofwegen's first email, I knew she was suffering deeply from losing her premature twins, Arie James and Hadilyn Faith. A friend had given her my grief book when she desperately needed someone to talk to who understood the pain of losing a child. Simultaneously, I received an invitation from my church to lead a small group to give hope to hurting women. I hesitated because of my schedule; however, when the woman calling said one of their leaders had just lost her best friend to a tragic accident and had signed up for this leaderless group, I sensed a door of opportunity opening. I agreed to be the group's leader and felt prompted to invite Shayla, even though I didn't know where she lived. To my surprise, I discovered she lived about an hour away from our church. Yet, she agreed to join us.

Our group's table was in the back corner of the large room with plenty of tissues and food. Dubbed the "Table of the Brokenhearted," our group members represented women suffering from a variety of life losses.

One group member was Andra Good. Her pain was raw and real from the recent loss of her best friend, Leigh Ann. Friends since childhood, Andra and Leigh Ann were both married and raising young children. Their families were enmeshed and celebrated birthdays and special occasions. Living life without Leigh Ann was incomprehensible for Andra. However, even in the midst of her deep heartache, her unwavering faith and trust in God shone through.

Together, our group passionately sought God's hope and truth. We lifted one another with God's Word, our presence, and prayer. One week after watching a Beth Moore video, we realized God placed us in the same field together for a season to sow deeply into one another and help one another grow.

Each week I saw growth happen. One week Shayla shared about her healing journey through her private blog.

"Have you ever considered making your blog public?" Andra asked.

Shayla looked surprised. The next week Shayla announced her "public" blog, and we celebrated the many posts she received from hurting women.

Another week, Andra announced her new ministry, Leigh's Blankies, created to honor her friend's life and carry on her love of children. Her vision was to sew blankets and provide them to children anywhere who needed comfort and hope. "I'm sending my first batch of blankies to an orphanage in Africa," she enthused. Soon after, another batch was sent to comfort tornado victims in Joplin, Missouri.

Then Shayla announced her vision to start Owl Love You Forever, a ministry to encourage grieving families who had lost a child. Her vision was to provide boxes of comfort to minister to moms in the hospital who had lost their baby. Her boxes would include practical items like a camera, a baggie for clips of hair, and two blankets: one for the baby to be wrapped in and a smaller one for the mom to keep.

Andra, Shayla, and I continued to meet during the next semester and opened our table to other hurting women. Ironically, we moved to the front of the room because I was invited to be the emcee for the entire group. I believe God opened this door of opportunity for me to use my platform to introduce others to our ministries and to mobilize others to help us spread hope to hurting women.

Many rallied to sew blankets. Others offered words of encouragement or prayers. Right before my bus trip for grieving moms, several women handed me money and gift cards to support the women on the trip. Amazingly, Shayla came on that bus to encourage others and has been coming ever since. Out of this web of relationships, ministries were born; physical, emotional, and spiritual needs were addressed; and hope was birthed.

God continues to amaze me. His healing power can transform broken hearts and use them to bring hope to others. He knows how to link every hurting heart with a heart that can offer hope and healing. Hope is a connection to the body of Christ, which has been commissioned to act as His hands and feet on this earth. Do you need this connection? Pray

He knows how to link every hurting heart with a heart that can offer hope.

for it, and God will send it to you. Do you have something to offer? Be alert and ready for the connections that God will send into your life. They may be common, everyday connections or mini-miracles. But God has orchestrated them for your mutual support. Find them, develop them, and celebrate them!

PART TWO

EMBRACING HOPE

CHAPTER 9

OVERCOMING HOPE BLOCKERS

Hope deferred makes the heart sick,
but a longing fulfilled is a tree of life.
—PROVERBS 13:12

The end of the long journey was in sight. The Israelites stood on the shore of the Jordan River. Finally, after forty years of trekking through the wilderness, it was time to possess the Promised Land. Victory was just a river crossing away. The only problem was the Jordan River was at flood stage. The fast-flowing, deep water was dangerous. With no ferry boats or life jackets in sight, swimming across was not an option for the sand dwellers. Hope was in view, just across the flooded river, but how would they overcome this seemingly impossible obstacle?

> *Hope blockers are obstacles that stop, block, or defer our ability to give hope to others.*
>
>

We already know the end to this story. God demonstrated His amazing power—"as soon as the priests who carried the ark reached the Jordan and their feet touched the water's edge, the water from upstream stopped flowing. It piled up in a heap a great distance away ... So the people crossed over ... on dry ground" (Joshua 3:15–17). God took what appeared to be an insurmountable obstacle and instead made it a sign of His grace and power.

Sooner or later in our journey to spread hope we will face our own Jordan River, or what I call *hope blockers: obstacles that stop, block, or defer our ability to give hope to others.* And these hope blockers are often numerous—and difficult! But before God can show us His miracle-working power, He sometimes has to reveal to us just what we're up against. He might force us to recognize some hope blockers, and to name them, before He will help us with them.

A Painting and a Post-It Note

I have a painting in my home of a woman standing at the bank of a river, gazing across the water to a cabin in the woods. Through the years I've imagined myself as the woman in the painting as I've faced challenges or seemingly impossible obstacles and longed to cross over to my promised land of hope.

While writing this book, I've made it a daily practice to look at the woman in the painting and ask the Holy Spirit to reveal anything that is blocking my hope or heart from trusting Him completely for that day. Whatever He revealed, I wrote down on a Post-it Note and stuck it on the painting. One extreme day, I glanced at the painting and realized I couldn't see the woman or the river because both were covered by multicolored sticky notes with scribbled negative words, like *doubt, fear,* and *anger.* Amazingly, God used this moment to bring laughter to me and transformed my dismal mood into a day of joy-filled writing with a clean heart.

God has turned many hopeless and hurtful situations in my life into victories. I want to pass on the hope I have received to others, but sometimes the hope I have to offer is blocked. In those moments I see myself as the woman in the painting facing a river of reasons for not reaching out to others. Let's look at some of those reasons.

Our Own Suffering

After losing our infant son, John Samuel, and three other babies through miscarriage, I remember looking at the painting and wondering, *Will I ever hold another living child?* Loss, grief, and infertility blocked my hope.

When a friend announced her pregnancy, I wrestled with silent envy and felt guilty for not being able to express wholehearted joy at her good news. For a season, baby showers and Mother's Day at church were occasions I dreaded. So I chose to guard my heart and not to attend either for a time, robbing my friends, and even God, of my presence and praise. Because I was so involved in my own suffering and grief, I did not have the emotional energy to help others, including my friend who needed me to listen when she was going through a crisis.

Suffering is a normal part of life, and for a time, it may block our ability to offer hope to others. Peter reminds us to expect seasons of trouble. "Dear friends, do not be surprised at the painful trial you are suffering, as though something strange were happening to you" (1 Peter 4:12 NIV 1984). But then he goes on to remind us that our suffering itself is doing a great work, and Jesus' glory will be revealed through it: "But rejoice that you participate in the sufferings of Christ, so that you may be overjoyed when His glory is revealed" (4:13).

At one point, a back injury caused me great suffering. When I was temporarily unable to walk and care for my family, God used my physical challenge to reveal hidden obstacles of pride, control, and patience I needed to face so I could allow others to help lift me, literally. For a season, my back injury blocked my ability to offer hope to others, but God's glory was revealed as He taught me to receive hope. If you are facing a season of suffering yourself, you may not be able to offer as much hope to others as you would like, but be assured, that time is not wasted. God will redeem that suffering, teaching you through the suffering or showing you the joy of receiving hope so that someday you can offer hope again to others.

Success

I've discovered that even good things, success, and positive circumstances may cause us pain and block our hope or ability to give it for a season. During an explosive season of ministry, my "to do" list and schedule were overwhelming. At one point, I had nearly three thousand unread emails. I found myself avoiding certain people, phone calls, or settings because I was unable to "do" more. I was hurting and discouraged inwardly, though outwardly it appeared I was doing well. I had to face my own hope blockers of too-high expectations, poor time management, and difficulty prioritizing before I could continue to spread hope to others. During that painful season, I learned to choose God's best for my life by enlisting people to pray and help me prioritize.

Likewise, I've discovered that joyous life events may limit our hope-giving for a time. When I was forty and Jake was ten, my doctor announced, "You're pregnant!" Although I was overjoyed at the news, fear was my obstacle. During each month of my pregnancy, I faced my fear and stepped in faith to the next month. Finally, after I had waited and persevered for two decades, God led the way for me to birth a living son, Joshua (Josh). Amazingly, two years later, another healthy son, Jordan, was born. And for several years my focus was primarily on my three sons and on writing, speaking, and preparing my heart to grow a business and ministry.

Positive events such as career success, marriage, the birth of a child, a new job opportunity, or a move may force us to focus on our own immediate needs. At those times, we should not feel guilty for our limitations. As a wise man noted, "There is a time for everything, and a season for every activity under the heavens" (Ecclesiastes 3:1). Your time for hope-giving will come again.

External Circumstances

Sometimes circumstances seemingly beyond our control can stop, block, or defer our ability to offer hope. A demanding job or busy family may limit your time and involvement with others. You may live too far away from the sufferer to offer the help you'd like. The amount or type of resources you have available to offer may seem too small or insignificant. Or, like my mom, you may have health issues or physical challenges that hinder you.

My mom won't admit to having Chronic Obstructive Pulmonary Disease (COPD) because she says it sounds like ownership and she doesn't want to call it hers. This progressive disease renders one unable to do simple things like having breath enough to walk more than a few feet, reach up, or exert limited energy in any way.

For most of her life my mom enjoyed an active lifestyle working, traveling, gardening, cooking, hunting, fishing, skiing, and serving her family, community, and church. However, over the past few years, her progressing health issues have forced her to adjust and become more creative in living and giving hope.

Now she faces her physical limitations by using a "handful of spoons," a concept she heard about that has given her hope to cope. Simply put, a handful of spoons represents one day's worth of her energy. It may take her two spoons to get up and three more to get dressed. Having limited energy causes Mom to prioritize her activities and say "no," to get the most out of her day before her spoons run out. This also includes making decisions about being a hopelifter and determining what she can do to offer hope to others. Prayer and encouraging others through phone calls, email, and listening are simple, less active ways she still spreads hope to others.

When Mom started using oxygen daily, she determined that with God's help, she would continue each day doing all she was physically able to do for as long as she could and be productive—which she still continues to this day, using the spoon concept. She is amazed how God gives her grace to persevere, and to also enjoy the journey. Mom has learned to "be content whatever the circumstance" (Philippians 4:11). By persevering and trusting God, she has learned the fruit of patience (which has never been a virtue of hers). God gives her a handful of spoons every morning and trusts her to use them well.

When external circumstances appear to block our efforts to help, that is our signal to stop, pray, and get connected to the Holy Spirit and His guidance. Sometimes the circumstance might be a signal from the Spirit that our involvement in the situation will have to be limited. We can't do it all. Not even Jesus could!

Sometimes, however, the external circumstances might be a wake-up call for you to shift your priorities and take care of something in your own life. For example, if clutter is hindering your ability to reach out, you'd best make it a priority to get your organization under control. I know of an inspiring, fruitful Christian woman whose hopelifting efforts are severely limited because of her lack of self-discipline and follow-through to get her clutter under control.

But sometimes the hope-blocking circumstance might simply call for an extra dose of creativity and fervent prayer.

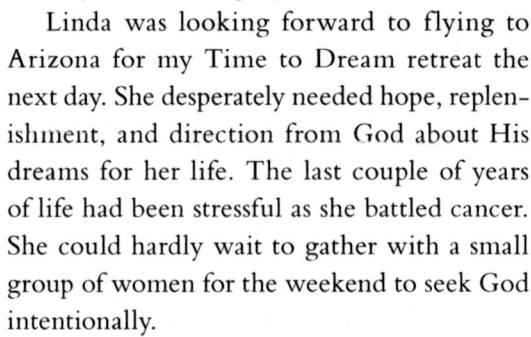

Hope-blocking circumstances call for an extra dose of creativity and fervent prayer.

Linda was looking forward to flying to Arizona for my Time to Dream retreat the next day. She desperately needed hope, replenishment, and direction from God about His dreams for her life. The last couple of years of life had been stressful as she battled cancer. She could hardly wait to gather with a small group of women for the weekend to seek God intentionally.

Amazingly, a friend had provided her airfare (or so she thought). But because of an extreme set of circumstances, she discovered the ticket was nonexistent. Tearful and disappointed, Linda realized she would not be going to Arizona.

When I received her early morning email sharing her sad news, I picked up the phone and called her. After listening to her share her disappointment and brainstorming possibilities, we realized this obstacle was too big for us to solve. So, I did what a hopelifter does: I prayed. I thanked God for the circumstance and praised him for this opportunity for him to reveal his miracle-working power and to part the water and make a way for Linda to come. We hung up trusting God to do the impossible.

Immediately, I emailed the other retreat participants asking them to join me in believing God would make a way for Linda to come and to join me in praising God. I imagined us like the Israelites at the edge of the flooded Jordan River facing this obstacle together as hopelifters. We joined forces through an email-led "cyberspace praise." "God, you are mighty ... You are a miracle worker ... You are our only Hope," I wrote.

What happened next still baffles me. It started with the thought, *Lay down your points.* Coincidentally, a few days earlier I had learned

OVERCOMING HOPE BLOCKERS

I had enough mileage points to fly to see my family. These points were precious to me, and I questioned if I would be a good steward to release them, knowing I would sacrifice this opportunity to see my family. So I asked God to clarify, and sensed Him say to my heart, "Are you afraid I won't come through for *your* ticket to see your family?"

I knew what I needed to do. I began searching for tickets to purchase with my points, but found none. So I called the airline and asked for their help. "You have a free ticket," I heard the agent say. I was confused. So I asked them to check again, and they confirmed I had a free ticket *and* points in my account.

Then she offered me several flight possibilities for the next day and put one on hold. Still not convinced and not wanting to disappoint Linda again, I hung up and called a different agent, only to receive the good news a third time! (Sounds like Peter.) This time, I asked the agent's name. "Angel," he said.

Only God could have orchestrated this. He not only provided a miracle ticket for Linda, but also for me, by removing the obstacle of unbelief in my heart and allowing me to keep my points for my ticket to see my family. The next time your hope is blocked, ask God to show you what the real hope blocker is and consider gathering a few friends to join you in a march of "Cyberspace praise." Then watch for His miracle-working power to do its work.

Internal Obstacles

Sometimes the toughest hope blockers to manage are not those that are outside us, but those that are *inside*. Our own thoughts, attitudes, and emotions can act as powerful barriers to reaching out. What we think about a person or their circumstances can shape our feelings and how we respond. We might look at someone in poverty and assume they are lazy or spending their money foolishly. But do we know the facts and truth about a person or situation, or are we judgmental or misinformed?

Another powerful internal blocker is self-doubt. *Their problem is too big for me. I don't think I can make a difference. Why me? Surely someone has more experience or could do a better job.* Sound familiar? Don't worry; we're not alone in our hesitation to help. Unbelief prevented a generation of Israelites from entering the Promised Land. Their lack of faith to believe God and look beyond the tangible to an intangible, unseen promise blocked their hope. We must guard our hearts and minds against doubting God and how He may choose to use us. Like the father who brought his son to Jesus to be healed and was rebuked by Jesus for his lack of faith, we need to cry out, "I do believe; help me overcome my unbelief!" (Mark 9:24). We too may need to invite Jesus to help us believe He can work through us to help others.

Another internal self-blocker could be our own high ideals and expectations. We might wish we could give a car to a family who needs one, but we can't afford that expense without jeopardizing our own family's needs. God might be asking us to help in a smaller way, offering a ride to church on Sunday or a weekly lift to the grocery store. Don't underestimate the Spirit's ability to connect and bless many small hopelifting efforts. He is a master of overcoming obstacles, both seen and unseen!

Another internal blocker to hope is fear. Fear can take a multitude of forms: fear of rejection, fear of failure, fear of doing or saying something wrong, fear of getting involved, fear of offending someone. While fear might sometimes be a signal that we should not get involved, I have found that most of the time my fears are not true, and when God gives me the green light to go ahead and help, I have learned to obey God and do it afraid. One day, I sensed the Holy Spirit prompting me to walk up to a complete stranger at a restaurant and tell her, "God loves you and hasn't forgotten you." I was afraid she would think I was crazy, but I did it anyway. Amazingly, I discovered she was suffering from a broken relationship and needed comfort. She also had attended our church youth group several years earlier and needed a timely invitation to return.

Pain can also block our efforts to extend hope. Frankly, sometimes helping others *hurts!* Visiting a grieving friend, watching a parent lose the battle against age and decay, or facing the scary symptoms of someone's addiction or mental illness may trigger feelings within us that are painful and cause us to suffer too. Yet our willingness simply to show up and suffer alongside someone is often the best hopelifting gift we can give. Jesus reminds us: "My command is this: Love each other as I have loved you" (John 15:12). Then He alerts us to the selfless quality of that love: "Greater love has no one than this: to lay down one's life for one's friends" (John 15:13). If we are going to be Christlike, sometimes we will need to suffer for our friends, as Christ did for us.

At times our unconfessed sin can also affect our ability to spread hope to others. Our unforgiveness, regret, anger, prayerlessness, judgmental attitude, or any number of other sins can halt the giving of hope. At times like this, when I sense that my own sin is holding me back, I simply ask the Holy Spirit to create in me a clean heart and renew a right spirit within me (Psalm 51:10).

> *The enemy of our soul does not want us to spread hope.*

Ultimately, all these obstacles, both external and internal, may be expressions of spiritual forces that are targeted against us. The enemy of our soul does not want us to spread hope. Paul reminds us, "For our struggle is not against flesh and blood, but against the rulers, against the authorities, against the powers of this dark world and against the spiritual forces of evil in the heavenly realms" (Ephesians 6:12). When my friends Hal and Cheryl Sacks of BridgeBuilders International felt called to help mobilize a strategic prayer effort for the border towns in California, Arizona, New Mexico, and Texas, they knew it would be difficult. Thousands joined them and engaged in unseen battles through prayer, which resulted in many victories.

Post-It Note Praise

I love God's creativity and tangible reminders of the hope He provides. When the Israelites crossed the Jordan River, He wanted them to remember this miracle moment and how He overcame the final obstacle that stood between them and the Promised Land. So He told them to take rocks from the middle of the dry river and build a memorial on the bank of the new land. As Joshua, their leader, told the people, "In the future when your descendants ask their parents, 'What do these stones mean?' tell them, 'Israel crossed the Jordan on dry ground.' For the LORD your God dried up the Jordan before you until you had crossed over … He did this so that all the peoples of the earth might know that the hand of the LORD is powerful and so that you might always fear the LORD your God" (Joshua 4:21–24).

Once God spoke to my heart as I looked at the painting of the woman standing before the river, and He told me *Remember Me and what I've done for you. Post it on the painting!*

So again, I picked up my Post-It notes and marker, but this time, instead of listing all my hope blockers, I began to write who God has revealed Himself to me to be: Deliverer. Healer. Hope. Companion. Strength. Transformer. Way. Truth. Rearguard. Commander of the Angel Armies. Victor. Miracle Worker. Peace. Daddy. Faithful Friend. Then I stuck every Post-It note on the bank of my river painting as an act of praise and thanksgiving, a personal memorial of praise.

Maybe you need to take a moment and read the story of the Israelites facing the flooded Jordan River. What is blocking your hope today? What is blocking your ability to spread hope to others? Review the list of internal and external hope blockers and invite the Holy Spirit to reveal to you what is blocking your hope and how He can help. Nothing is impossible with Him. He is willing and able to overcome any obstacle. Put your hope in Him, remembering who He is and what He has already done. Then build Him a memorial of praise.

CHAPTER 10

HOPELIFTERS NEED HOPE TOO

Therefore encourage one another and build
each other up, just as in fact you are doing.
—1 THESSALONIANS 5:11

Hopelifters need hopelifters too!

We need others to lift us up, provide support, and keep us growing so we can continue to spread hope to others. God created us as part of the body of Christ with unique gifts, talents, and life experiences to serve and support one another. Even Jesus, the ultimate Hopelifter, was intentional about giving and receiving support. He invited twelve men to work with him in His ministry to spread hope to a hurting world. And women like Mary and Martha offered Him hospitality, friendship, and times of rest.

> *Developing a personal network of support starts with knowing who God created you to be.*

Having a willing spirit to not only give, but also to receive support from others can help you become a more effective hopelifter. Developing a personal network of support starts with knowing who God created you to be and what your unique roles and needs are.

Know Your Unique Roles

"What do your hands bring to the family of God?"

I looked at the diverse group of women and could hardly wait to hear their answers to my question. I handed each of them a piece of paper and directed them to trace their hand and write down five things about themselves. Then they took turns sharing their unique life experiences, talents, gifts, and passions. I was amazed at the variety of their answers. To experience the body of Christ connecting with one another and observe God's power at work through every part exhilarates me. Watching Him link together a woman with a passion for prayer sitting next to a woman in need of it, or women with shared-life experiences who can support one another beyond the workshop, energizes me. God has used this simple exercise time and time again to encourage countless lives by providing them the opportunity to know and connect with other parts and roles in the body of Christ.

Then I asked, "What roles do you have in your life?"

Before they could respond, I held up my three-ring binder with a photocopy of my hands on it. Most of the women looked perplexed.

"I have to keep life simple, so I've decided I can have only ten roles," I said as I pointed to my ten fingers on the cover. The women erupted into laughter.

Then I shared my roles for that season written on my fingers on the cover:

Child of God	Friend/neighbor
Self-Care	Communicator
Wife	Creator
Mother	Connector
Family Member	Organizational Leader

Although my roles have changed throughout the years, I've maintained my ten-role limit. By focusing my energy on fewer roles, I'm able to be a more effective hopelifter.

I learned this the hard way during a fruitful season of ministry when I didn't know how to say no. At that time I was leading a nonprofit ministry and had recently suffered the loss of our son. I found relief from my grief by doing more, but some might say I was "missing in action." One day after "forgetting" another important appointment, I knew I needed to evaluate. To my shock I discovered I was juggling twenty-seven roles in my life. With the help of my board and a wise adviser, Carol Travilla, author of *Caring Without Wearing*,[10] I became more intentional about embracing my most important roles and released many responsibilities to others. It was a process of letting go and finding the right balance for who I am.

For now, ten has worked as my number, but you may have fewer roles or perhaps more than ten. Perhaps the simple act of listing your own roles may help you to clarify what you do and where God is calling you to use your gifts.

Developing One Role at a Time

Inside my three-ring binder with my photocopied hands are sheets that include dreams and goals for each role. This system worked well for many years; however, my needs changed, so I expanded this concept. Now, I have ten binders and ten baskets, one of each for every role. My binders still have dreams and goals, and I've also added a prayer and journal section. Meanwhile, the baskets store resources like books, articles, brochures, coupons, and gifts for each role. (Perhaps someday I will store them some other creative way.)

Because I get distracted easily, this current system helps me focus on one role at a time. It's easy and fun to pick up a binder or basket and focus on a smaller part of who I am.

One day, I realized the pages in my binder for my wife role were mostly blank and my basket was empty. I asked God to forgive me for neglecting this role. I invited the Holy Spirit to teach me how to be a more intentional wife and to fill me and my binder and basket with his promises, people, and practical resources.

If you were to review your roles, what would be your dreams and goals for each one? (Goals should be specific, measurable, attainable, and realistic, and have a time listed by which to complete them.) What resources will help you develop added strength and skill in those roles? Begin to collect ideas: books, websites, conferences, contacts. Then have fun nurturing those roles!

Redefining and Releasing Roles

During seasons of suffering or increased demands, we may need to release specific roles or redefine them. For a time, Moses' leadership of the Israelites required that he act as a judge. When judging disputes became too demanding for Moses, his father-in-law said, "What you are doing is not good. You and these people who come to you will only wear yourselves out. The work is too heavy for you; you cannot handle it alone" (Exodus 18:17–18). Moses took his advice, trained others, and released much of that work to them.

We may need to release specific roles or redefine them.

While writing this book, I quickly realized I couldn't maintain all of my roles well. I was overwhelmed, and my expectations were unrealistic. My life coach, Anne Denmark of Life Discovery Coaching, helped me prioritize and develop a plan to redefine my roles and release responsibility to others for a season. By rescheduling my work assignments and by enlisting help for meals, driving, and administrative support, I added several hours a week to my writing time during a critical few weeks.

Sometimes through loss or other life circumstances, we may be forced to release a role entirely. During these times we may discover new opportunities to grow. After my uncle died, my Aunt Don added "art student" to her roles. Although she missed her role as wife, she experienced enjoyment in her new role and all the new activities, people, and creativity it brought to her life.

Fill Your Pitcher

"How do you fill your pitcher?" I'll never forget hearing the speaker's words as she finished pouring water into several glasses and held up an empty pitcher. I could relate to feeling empty after pouring myself out to others. She challenged everyone to find simple ways to "fill our pitcher." My list included:

- Spending time with God
- Reading a book or Scripture
- Conversation with a friend
- Going to the river, mountains, or cool weather
- Treating myself to a latte
- Taking a night off from laundry or cooking
- Creating an event or fun experience
- Visiting my mom and eating her pie

Nurturing myself is still difficult for me. Yet I know from personal experience that when I don't, I'm unable to pour out hope to others as well as I could. I've also discovered that spending time with God always fills my pitcher.

Even Jesus recognized His need for personal replenishment. He was intentional about getting away to rest and pray after working hard in His roles of teacher, healer, and miracle worker. Spending time alone with the Father always filled Him up. He was also alert to the needs of his disciples. Mark reports that after a busy season of ministry, "the apostles gathered around Jesus and reported to Him all they had done and taught. Then, because so many people were coming and going that they did not even have a chance to eat, He said to them, 'Come with me by yourselves to a quiet place and get some rest.' So they went away by themselves in a boat to a solitary place" (Mark 6:30–32). Did you notice how Jesus protected them from working too much? From the beginning of time, God built into our weeks a time for work and for Sabbath rest. So don't feel afraid or guilty if you need to rest. If you don't take the rest, your body will eventually *force* you to take it, by getting sick.

List ways you can nurture yourself. Your ways will not be the same as anyone else's—one woman might need a loud, energetic zumba class, while another needs a quiet walk alone. One woman might need to curl up with a good book, while another might crave dinner and a movie with friends. Whatever fills you, replenishes you, and nourishes you is worth fitting into your routine.

People Before You: Mentors for Life

"You need people before you, beside you, and behind you to succeed."

How I needed to hear these timely words. The luncheon speaker had triggered an issue in my life: my need for support. It was the 1980s, and I had just left my media career to pioneer a nonprofit ministry for Christian business and professional women. At that time most churches did not offer programs or practical support for workplace women. Many women like myself felt alone and misunderstood as we tried to live our faith at work. Although I had no idea how to lead a workplace ministry and was leary of women's groups, I knew God had called me to serve this unique group of professional Christian women. With great enthusiasm and passion, I encouraged business and professional women to live their faith at work.

As I asked myself, "Who is before me?" I looked around and realized I needed mentors to help *me* grow. I took our speaker's advice to talk to God that day. I penned a lengthy letter to Him and at the bottom I wrote: "P.S. GOD, COULD YOU PLEASE SEND SOMEONE TO HELP ME SPEAK, PRAY, AND WRITE?"

Amazingly, He answered my prayer through a series of connections that started with a book a friend gave me. My plan to read for an hour turned into an all-night reading binge, which resulted in my calling the author early the next morning and inviting her to Arizona. To my surprise and delight, she said "yes."

When I first met Carol Kent, she had laryngitis and was forced to listen to *me* at my kitchen counter during a significant crossroads in my life and ministry. I discovered she was also the founder of a Christian communication training seminar called Speak Up With Confidence. Our God connection quickly blossomed into a long-distance friendship, mentoring, and ministry relationship. I had no idea the significant roles of givers and receivers of hope we would be for one another through the years, including such events as the death of my baby and the life incarceration of Carol's only son, Jason.

With Carol's urging, I flew to Michigan to attend my first Speak Up seminar. Ironically, she invited *me* to serve as a facilitator, encouraging others who wanted to speak. I was definitely out of my comfort zone. One participant I met was Marlae Gritter, a passionate Michigan prayer director at the time, overseeing several hundred prayer groups for Moms in Touch International (now Moms in Prayer International). I had never heard of this ministry; however, when she shared their mission to pray for their children and schools, Marlae and I became fast friends. She encouraged me from afar when I started leading a Moms in Touch group for our school and helped plan a statewide rally to mobilize other moms to pray.

My passion for training speakers spread, and our workplace ministry brought Speak Up to Arizona. That's how God connected me to Cheryl Sacks, a prayer movement leader and cofounder of Bridge-Builders International, who became another mentor for me in prayer. She taught me the importance of bringing prayer first in everything and the secret of becoming intentional and strategic about enlisting others to pray for me in my ministry. Her PIT Team strategy changed my life. (More about that later in this chapter.)

God also used my connection with Carol Kent to deliver a writing mentor. Carol introduced Judith Couchman to me when she learned about Judith's involvement in a Christian leadership network for professional women, and Judith invited me to a writer's retreat. Our God connection was timely. Sadly, when I flew to Colorado Springs for the retreat, I was grieving the recent loss of my infant son. A short time later, Judith connected me to an editor at Zondervan when they were looking for a grief devotional writer, and they contracted me to write my first two books.

Hopelifters need a network of support.

Hopelifters need a network of support. When we cry out to God to provide, He will. I'm thankful to Him for sending Carol Kent, Marlae Gritter, Cheryl Sacks, and Judith Couchman, *women before me*, who have helped me speak, pray, and write. Who are the people before you who have offered wisdom and resources to help you grow? Take a moment and thank God for them. In what area of your life do you need someone before you today to help you grow? Tell God your needs and be ready to respond to His answer.

For example, when the virgin Mary discovered she was pregnant, she reached out to her cousin, Elizabeth, who was also experiencing a miraculous pregnancy. How comforted Mary must have felt to spend time with another pregnant woman carrying a special child and to have the freedom to ask questions and share concerns. God always provides others before us who understand and can offer comfort and support, whether in person, online, or in the pages of a book of the Bible.

People Beside You: Friends in the Fire

When the doctor announced "Your baby is going to die!" I needed friends beside me to help me through the next twenty-eight weeks of my pregnancy (recall my story from chapter 6). Amazingly, God hand-picked two friends, Lisa Jernigan and Jan James, to be with me in my journey. I call them "my friends in the fire." Like Shadrach, Meshach, and Abednego, who were thrown into the fire together when they wouldn't renounce their faith (Daniel 3), my friends willingly journeyed with me into the flames of suffering and took a stand with me for God's miracle-working power.

God unleashed his creativity and compassion through this dynamic duo during my several-month journey of carrying and losing my son. My precious friends became the hands and feet of Jesus and taught me how to receive well. They rallied prayer support and card campaigns, accompanied me to doctor visits, planned a shower, wore matching T-shirts as my waiting room greeters, and—before the days of cell phones and social networking—set up a communication strategy for friends and family during my labor and delivery. Amazingly, Jan and her husband, Greg, even shared her birthday and their anniversary (both on August 22) with hats and cake in my labor room. My friends held my precious baby and celebrated his short life with me. Lisa and Jan even spoke at the praise celebration to thank God publicly for our son. I will never forget my friends' willingness, availability, and creativity. My fearless friends pointed me to God and lifted my hope when I desperately needed it.

We all need people beside us for reasons or seasons, companions who trek through happy or hard times and share laughter or tears. Joshua and Caleb spied together, stood in faith, and possessed the Promised Land together. Paul and Barnabas spread the gospel together. Women watched Jesus die at the foot of the cross together, and they also went to the tomb early in the morning together. Even Jesus needed friends beside Him. He invited Peter, James, and John to pray with Him and share His sorrow in the garden before He was arrested and crucified.

Who is beside you in your journey? Who are your friends in the fire? Thank God for them. Send them a "thank you" card, text, or call. Or invite God to reveal a person who needs a friend and then reach out.

People Behind You: Help for the Hurting

We're always a few steps ahead of someone. Reaching back to help someone who needs our strength, expertise, or experience keeps us challenged to keep growing. Investing in others can also spread hope in greater ways.

"I don't understand why all of this has to happen," sobbed my friend. Her heart was breaking from the loss of her husband and several other disappointments. My heart ached for my suffering friend. Although my life experiences were different than hers, I could relate to some of her pain. I had endured many times of questioning God, disappointment, unmet expectations, and unforgiveness. During those times, God provided people who reached out, listened, wiped my tears, and pointed me gently to His truth. This was my opportunity to pass on what others had offered to me. *God, use me to lead her to hope again!* I prayed silently.

Coincidentally, it was raining outside as cleansing tears flowed inside. I could sense God's healing happening as I listened to her pour out her hurts, and we talked and prayed together.

"I believe God will use you to comfort others," I said as I hugged her good-bye. Ironically, when she left, the rain had stopped too.

Anything you offer God can be used to help others less fortunate than you or behind you in their journey. Even your past pain can be a blessing to someone. Hopelifters are willing to reach back and pass hope on.

Who is behind you in the journey? Who is someone a few steps behind you in their faith, life stage, or ability to cope with a situation? Is someone going through what you've already experienced? Pray and ask God to show you someone who needs what you have. Then be ready to offer a service, an expertise, or an experience to that person.

Wise Advisors: Your Personal Board of Directors

A few years ago a conference director asked me to speak on "balance." I graciously declined because I struggled with this topic. She assured me she wanted *me*, because of my weakness and willingness to be authentic and transparent. I was surprised, but accepted this challenging assignment. As I prepared for the workshop, God inspired me with the idea to create a team of wise advisors to help in decision making for that season. I realized churches have elders and leadership teams, organizations have boards, even King Arthur had the Knights of the Round Table, so why shouldn't I have a team? I needed others to help me make wise choices, provide accountability, and help me fulfill my God-given potential.

As I prayed about my first potential team of support, God brought to mind names of people for each of my roles. I emailed them an invitation asking them to provide advice and counsel to me for the next six months during a critical season of decision making. I was unprepared for their enthusiastic responses. I sent them an overview of my God-given purpose, spiritual gifts, passions, schedule, opportunities, and challenges. It helped guide them through situations where advice was needed. Their accountability also enabled my spontaneous personality to pause and say to myself and others, "I need to get input from my personal board." My wise advisors, then and now, help me say "yes" to the best things and "no" to many good opportunities.

Every season of our life brings different challenges. You may be early in your faith journey, marriage, or career, nearing the end of your life, or somewhere in between. Even if you don't feel you need lots of advisors, perhaps one or two could help you through decision making about a life-challenging situation. God may want to use their gift. You never know how encouraged they may feel when you value who they are. By receiving, you may be giving in disguise.

In what areas of your life do you need wise advisors? Pray and ask God to reveal possible people. Determine your expectations and guidelines for their help. Then reach out and ask!

Partners in Prayer: Your PIT Team

"Do you have a PIT Team?"

When my mentor-in-prayer Cheryl Sacks first posed this question, I was dumbfounded. Then she revealed its hidden meaning: *Personal Intercessory Team.*

Sure, I had a few people praying for me, but at that time prayer was more of an afterthought, not a strategic, intentional effort like Cheryl was challenging me to have in my life. She pointed to the example of Moses, Aaron, and Hur as a PIT team model:

> So Joshua fought the Amalekites as Moses had ordered, and Moses, Aaron and Hur went to the top of the hill. As long as Moses held up his hands, the Israelites were winning, but whenever he lowered his hands, the Amalekites were winning. When Moses' hands grew tired, they took a stone and put it under him and he sat on it. Aaron and Hur held his hands up — one on one side, one on the other — so that his hands remained steady till sunset. So Joshua overcame the Amalekite army with the sword. (Exodus 17:10–13)

Make prayer your highest priority.

Cheryl's reminder of God's truth to make prayer my highest priority and to enlist others to lift up their hands and fight spiritual forces on my behalf has transformed my life and ministry. In true hopelifter style, I've passed on what I learned from Cheryl and Moses to others. Each time I give someone a copy of Cheryl's book *The Prayer Saturated Church*, I'm reminded of

God's faithfulness in answering my prayer to send someone to grow me in prayer.

Behind the pages of this book are unseen heroes, my PIT team. I enlisted them specifically to pray for me during the process of my writing this book. Most weeks, I sent them an email update of my praises and prayer needs. In times of personal crisis, I called or texted more often. My PIT team's prayers have lifted me through multiple challenges and times of doubt and discouragement so I could win the battle and finish victoriously. They've also prayed for you, my reader, and those you will spread hope to.

Who is lifting you in prayer? If you already have a PIT team, how could you be more intentional? If you don't have one, ask God to show you who could pray for you. Then determine your group's guidelines. How will you communicate with them and share your answers and needs? Or, could God be calling you to be "Moses" for someone else and pray more intentionally?

I'll say it again: hopelifters need hopelifters. We need others to lift us up, provide support, and keep us growing so we can continue to spread hope to others. As you review your roles and look for ways to grow, also be alert to God's ways of supporting you. Rest from busy seasons and find ways to replenish yourself. Look for people before you, beside you, and behind you in the journey. Surround yourself with wise advisors and prayer partners. As they lift you up, you too will gain strength to lift others.

CHAPTER 11

DEVELOPING YOUR HOPE PLAN

May the God of hope fill you with all joy and peace as you trust in Him, so that you may overflow with hope by the power of the Holy Spirit.

—ROMANS 15:13

I once heard someone say, "Spreading hope to hurting people gives others a glimpse of God." When we listen to an aching soul, offer our shoulder to lean on, or provide creative help, we reveal Jesus and become His hands and feet.

Daily opportunities abound to encourage family members, friends, coworkers, neighbors, and strangers in need of God's touch. Seeing needs and responding to them in meaningful ways can be energizing, fulfilling, and humbling.

Your hopelifting will look different than mine. Just as your personality and purpose is unique, so are the people you'll touch and the hope you will offer. Hopelifting is an ongoing process of discovery. It's important to steward well what God has entrusted to us so we are ready to respond to spread hope when He calls.

Who do you know that needs hope? Does that person need hope for a moment, during a season, or through a crisis, or do they need long-term strategic hope? Developing a hope plan can help you become more effective. Much like a recipe, a hope plan helps you recognize and prepare the resources God has entrusted to you, so you can respond with creative compassion, using just the right ingredients.

Ready Your Heart

Before you can create a plan, however, you first need to ready your heart. Pray to God to show you when and where He wants to use you. I love the simple prayer that my friend Sandy Austin uses: "Lord, break my heart with what breaks Yours."

I met Sandy when she was working for a ministry to athletes and began attending our Christian Business Women's luncheons in Arizona. Sandy stood out. She was the only one who wore shorts and polo shirts to our meetings. Sandy's smile, sense of humor, deep passion for Jesus, and compassionate heart was even more noticeable. When God prompted Sandy to send me a handwritten note of encouragement, I was hurting deeply as a new leader. Sandy's timely words helped me persevere and sparked our friendship.

Before you can create a plan, you need to ready your heart.

When Sandy announced her move to Colorado to embrace a new job as a high school counselor, I was sad to lose her, but I was excited for my friend. I knew God had a purpose and plan for her. Then on April 20, 1999, Sandy received an urgent call requesting her help as an onsite high school counselor after the tragic Colorado school shooting. She rushed to the designated building where families were gathering to learn the fate of their sons and daughters. Her presence, listening ear, words, and prayers were needed at this time of deep pain and fear. Sandy was there with a compassionate heart as the hands and feet of Jesus. She rejoiced when students were reunited with their families. After several hours of waiting with two families, it was eventually confirmed that their children were among the twelve students killed. God chose Sandy to be His comforter and counselor to hurting people in a significant time of crisis.

Sandy's example inspires me to keep praying for a compassionate heart, "Lord, break my heart with what breaks Yours." Will you join us? Ask God where He wants to use you. He will show you!

Ready Your Resources

What hope can you offer? Perhaps it's time for a hope audit. Invite the Holy Spirit to open your eyes to the many ways you can spread hope. We started to look at our resources in chapter 7, "Hope in a Possession." Here's another way to look at what we have: Our resources include not only the tangible—which are easy to see, touch, and list—but also the intangible. Consider the following possibilities:

Tangible Resources

What tangible resources do you own or have access to that could bring others hope? This could include a variety of things: home, car, spare room, bicycle, computer, tools, craft materials, furniture, clothing, bedding, books, sports gear, and more. You may not be called to "give the shirt off your back" (although I have, but that's another story), but God does ask us to act as faithful stewards of His gifts—not burying them or hoarding them, but putting them to good use to advance his kingdom (see the parable of the talents in Matthew 25:14-30). Sometimes, we won't realize we have something that someone else needs until the need pops up! Or until God asks us to do something with that resource, as He did when He prompted me to sell a bed on Craigslist (see the story in chapter 4).

Intangible Resources

Besides the tangible resources God has blessed you with, He has also equipped you with a multitude of intangible resources. First and foremost, the Holy Spirit is your source for power, truth, and direction. The Holy Spirit entrusts you with spiritual gifts, such as the gift of hospitality or teaching (see 1 Corinthians 12). Your life experiences, whether good or bad, are another intangible resource you can offer.

Look at your education or special training. How does it equip you to serve? What work or volunteer experience do you have? Can that background be used in another area? What special skills, natural talents, or expertise do you possess (for example, technology, writing,

speaking, carpentry, cooking, gardening, parenting, singing, organizing). Could you use that skill or expertise to help someone?

What is your personality? Do you enjoy helping someone one-
on-one, or in a group setting? Do you prefer leadership and executive roles or behind-the-scenes helping? How does your personality
end up influencing where and how you give hope?

What are your connections? What groups, organizations, or ministries are you connected with? What expertise or support could they
offer? Who are your work colleagues, family, or friends? Perhaps one
of them could be put in touch with the hurt-
ing person you know. Even people you don't
personally know can be resources—authors,
speakers, pastors, bloggers, and musicians can
minister to the hurting through a book, radio,
conference, or online.

> *All of us have
> a unique set
> of both tangible
> and intangible
> resources.*

All of us have a unique set of tangible and
intangible resources. So don't compare or
worry if you don't have Person A's wealth or
Person B's education or Person C's personal-
ity. God created you for a unique hopelifting role that cannot be
duplicated by anyone else. As Paul reminds us: "For we are God's
workmanship, created in Christ Jesus to do good works, which God
prepared in advance for us to do" (Ephesians 2:10). Isn't that a wonderful thought? We are God's special handiwork, and He has already
planned out the good works He wants us to do. It is only up to us to
watch for His promptings, and then to respond.

Hope for a Lifetime

There is one more precious intangible resource that deserves a category all its own: your time. Have you considered the timing and
duration of your hopelifting efforts? Some hopelifting requires a
lifetime commitment, as in the case of marriage and family. Our
parents, spouse, children, and other close relatives should always be
at the top of our list of people we need to lift up, and we must be
careful not to neglect their needs even as we minister to others. Paul

even adds a caution to that effect: "Anyone who does not provide for their relatives, and especially for their own household, has denied the faith and is worse than an unbeliever" (1 Timothy 5:8). While Paul is likely speaking of financial provision here, we all know families who are financially well off but starved for emotional or spiritual support. Are you sure you are providing those precious resources to your family?

I believe one of the most important tasks of Christian parents is to be lifelong intercessors for our children, like my friends Gene and Carol Kent. Their only son, Jason, is serving a life sentence without the possibility of parole in a Florida prison. Despite his circumstances, Jason is committed to spread God's hope to hurting inmates for the rest of his life. I believe he is able to spread hope because of God's power and because he has parents who support him spiritually with prayer and emotionally with calls, letters, and visits.

So, take a moment to look at your lifetime commitments. Are you careful to prioritize the needs of your immediate family? If not, you may need to scale back on your other commitments for a time as you focus on them.

Hope for a Season

The wise writer of Ecclesiastes tells us there are times and seasons for everything. Seasons may vary in purpose, duration, and intensity. Mary spent a season of her life raising Jesus and His siblings. Jesus spent a season of three years in His public ministry mentoring His disciples and spreading hope. Later, Paul spent more than half his life—over thirty years—spreading the gospel through his travels and letters. Seasons may be short or long, but what's important is being alert to how God is calling you to use your time during that season.

> *Our hopelifting efforts will take different forms during different seasons of our lives.*

Our hopelifting efforts will take different forms during different seasons of our lives. During a season of singleness, God may use us to minister to other single friends. During a season of career, God may ask to us to focus on developing our skills and sharing them with others. During a season of retirement, God may open new volunteer opportunities we'd never considered before. If you find yourself frustrated by the limitations of your current season, let God remind you of how He has used you in the past, and ask Him to inspire you with a vision of different ways He may use you in the future. You don't have to do everything now. To everything there is a season.

Besides looking at our own time commitments and what season of life we are experiencing, it is also important to look at the person you are hoping to help. You will need to understand the person's needs, what is needed, and for how long before you commit. A person in a season of deep suffering may need hopelifters who are available to listen, help make decisions, or serve in simple ways like cooking and cleaning. People with the spiritual gifts of mercy and service usually show up here. One woman adopted a hurting person for a year. She bought a year's worth of cards, organized them in a pocket calendar, and mailed them on significant anniversaries, dates, and holidays. Her actions demonstrated the spiritual gift of encouragement.

Like a runner pressing through the pain of a marathon, someone who is in a season of persevering may need a hopelifter who can encourage and affirm her forward and help her see beyond her situation to the bigger picture. When my husband lost his job and was unemployed, a few people stepped in to pray, call, and encourage, and they provided job leads and job search savvy. One friend surprised us by purchasing us a dishwasher we couldn't afford when ours broke at that time.

Who do you think God might be calling you to reach?

Some people may need help as they go through a season of character building. Internal change, refining, and pruning usually happens during this season. A person may need a hopelifter with wisdom and discernment and a more mature faith to help them determine priorities and discover new directions. For example, with the help of her sister, a woman came to realize her codependent patterns that enabled her husband's addictions, and her sister supported her as she developed new boundaries to address his misbehavior.

Try to describe your current season in life. What are you doing, and who are you already helping? Who do you think God might be calling you to reach? What is their situation, how can you help, and how much time can you commit to help them? Not all hopelifting efforts take a lifetime, or even a season. As you will see below, hope sometimes only takes a moment.

Hope for a Moment

Each twenty-four-hour period has 86,400 seconds. It takes only a few seconds to smile at someone, give a hug, say "I'm praying for you," mail a card, or hand a homeless person bottled water.

Most mornings before work, I stop for coffee and start my day on "holy grounds" with God. I envision Him sitting at the table across from me as I read my Bible or devotion. I make it a daily practice to share insights from my moments spent with Him. A quick text or online post can spread hope and help others enjoy a moment with Him too. Instead of wasting time when I'm waiting in line at the store or a fast food drive-thru, or sitting in a doctor's office, I pull out my phone and spend those moments praying for people in my contacts. As I scroll down the list of names, I spread hope by lifting that person to God. When I click on my husband and three sons' names, I have several Scriptures I've carefully chosen and typed in so I can easily pray for the specific need they have. Instead of wasting time waiting, use those moments to pray.

Take a moment right now to spread hope to someone. Phone it. Mail it. Text it. Post it. Pray it.

Hope for a Reason

What is the specific reason someone needs hope?

Do they need timely advice or a skill you have to offer? Is the anniversary of the death of their loved one approaching? Do they

need help moving or money to pay for storage? Would a ride to chemotherapy bring them hope? One simple act for the right reason can
bring hope to hurting people.

> *A hopelifter looks for people in need of hope.*

People in need of hope are everywhere.
Some are easier to spot, like homeless people,
those with physical challenges, or parents
yelling at their children. Others may suffer
silently from hidden hurt, secret shame, or
success, although outwardly they look fine. A
hopelifter looks for people in need of hope.

"Before a person can communicate compassion, he or she must
see another's woundedness and be saddened by it," Carol Kent wrote
in *Becoming a Woman of Influence*.[11]

In the movie *Patch Adams*, actor Robin Williams is determined to
become a medical doctor because he enjoys helping people. Unfortunately, the medical and scientific community do not embrace
his creative approach to bring compassion and comfort to patients.
When he visits a dreary hospital ward full of sick children, he realizes
their greatest need is cheering up. He transforms an aspirator bulb
into a clown's nose, a bedpan into a cowboy hat, and pretends to ride
an IV stand like a bucking bronco. Laughter erupts and spreads to all
of the children in the room.

Pause for a moment and trade places in your mind with the person you want to help. What is she experiencing? What are the facts
about the situation? In what role of her life is she hurting (child of
God, wife, mother, employee)? What is her obvious need? Emotional? Physical? Relational? Financial? Spiritual? What hidden needs
does she have? If she has multiple needs in many different areas, pray
that God will use you to address one or more of her needs, and trust
(and pray) that he will use others to take care of the rest.

Types of Hope

Sometimes the hope we spread to others may be anonymous, while
other times we will work face-to-face. Some hopelifting might be
spontaneous, while other hopelifting may be strategic. All types of

hope are welcome, as you will see in the examples and stories that follow.

Anonymous Hope

Spreading secret hope can be meaningful and fun, for the giver or receiver. Sometimes when I go through the drive-thru I tell the cashier, "I'll pay for the person behind me." I like the idea of spreading hope to an unsuspecting stranger in the car behind me. I ask the cashier to tell the person, "God loves you. It's a gift from him."

> *Some hopelifting might be spontaneous, while other hopelifting may be strategic.*

One day during a discouraging season of transition in my life, the doorbell rang. When I opened the door no one was there. I thought I was the victim of a prank and then I saw it: a small gift bag sitting on my doorstep. To my surprise when I peeked inside, I found a variety of encouraging items, including a CD and a card that was signed:

Love,
C.H.R.I.S.T.

As I discovered, C.H.R.I.S.T. is an acronym meaning Caring Helpers Reaching Individuals Sharing Treasures. I'm grateful to God for prompting someone to be His hands and feet and spread anonymous hope in a bag when I really needed it. While most hopelifting involves face-to-face contact, sometimes God asks us to give to the needy so secretly, so anonymously, that our left hand should not even know what our right hand is doing (Matthew 6:3)!

Spontaneous Hope

God may prompt us to spread hope spontaneously. When he does, be ready.

For example, a few years after my son died, I felt led to go to the cemetery to spend time with God. *Take one of your grief books with you to the cemetery.* I knew God was planting this crazy thought, so I did it. When I arrived, I sat down on the bench near my son's grave, closed my eyes, and listened. A bird chirped. Leaves rustled in the gentle breeze. Water trickled from a nearby fountain. Then I heard a muffled cry. Who could it be?

I opened my eyes and saw a young woman standing by a freshly dug grave. Immediately, I felt impressed to go talk to her. I learned the woman's young son had recently died.

"I'm so sorry for your loss," I said. "God loves you and I believe He sent me here today to tell you and give you this."

When I handed her my book, she shook her head and swiped a tear from her cheek.

"I was alone here and didn't know what to do, so I prayed, 'God, if you're real, please help me!' Then you showed up!" she said.

We continued to talk, and I told her my story and showed her my son's grave. We talked about heaven, our boys being playmates, and then I asked if she wanted to know with certainty that she would see her son again. She said, "Yes!" Amazingly, in a place of death, we rejoiced in eternal life. I'm so thankful I responded to a crazy God-thought and spread spontaneous hope to a woman in crisis who cried for help.

Be alert to spontaneous moments when you can spread hope. You will be amazed at how God can take mere moments of your time to spread hope to those in need.

Systematic Hope

Sometimes, of course, organization or a methodical way of spreading hope may be appropriate. When a circumstance or need is extreme, mobilizing others to help us in a more deliberate effort may be necessary. I discovered that truth in 1999 when I had an unexpected visit from my friends, Gene and Carol Kent.

"Kathe, I have something to tell you," sighed Carol. "I waited to tell you in person."

I gazed at my two somber-looking friends. Gene clutched Carol's hand. I sensed something was terribly wrong. During the next several minutes, Carol tearfully recalled the devastating details that led to her only son's arrest for murder.

This can't be true! I thought. Disbelief gripped me as I plummeted to the depths of shock. Though I desperately wanted to throw my heartbroken friends a line of hope, I knew my words could not remove their unthinkable pain. Instead, I offered my silence, my tears, and my prayers.

Over the next several days I cried out to God on behalf of my friends. I longed to "do" something, but I didn't know where to begin. I knew this situation was too big for my friends to shoulder.

I asked God to unleash his creativity through *me* to support Gene and Carol. And he did. Over the next few days, ideas flooded my mind.

When I asked Carol's blessing to mobilize support for her, I sensed her reluctance at first. I understood how receiving support is much harder than giving it. However, I also knew from my own experience there are times and seasons for both. I believed this was Gene and Carol's season to receive (apparently others were telling them the same thing). To my relief and delight, they finally agreed.

"Kathe, other friends have also contacted me about mobilizing support. Perhaps you can work together!" Carol said.

Within a few days, we met by phone, teamed up, and started to mobilize and administer strategic support for the Kent family. Over the next two and a half years leading up to their son, Jason's, trial, we witnessed God's creative compassion in action through people throughout the United States and Canada. Every suggestion made to support Carol, Gene, Jason, his wife, step-daughters, and extended family was met or exceeded. Holidays, birthdays, anniversaries, and trials (there were seven postponements) were remembered in meaningful ways. Some traveled to offer their ministry of presence, while most offered support from afar. Although years have passed since Jason's life imprisonment, many continue to support the Kent family through their nonprofit prison ministry, *Speak Up For Hope*. Now I understand at a deeper level what the Bible means when it says to comfort those with the comfort you have received. I've also learned how important it is to invite others to help us spread hope.

Who are a few people (or organizations) you could ask to help you carry the load to help someone during an extreme season? What will you ask them to do?

Your Hopelifting Plan

As you develop your own personal hopelifting plan, remember to pray first to ask God to work in your heart to reveal who needs your help. Then ready your resources: assess both the tangible and the intangible assets God has blessed you with, so that when those resources are called upon, you will be ready to offer them. Keep in mind how much time is needed for hopelifting efforts and what you can give. What are your lifetime commitments, and are you honoring them? What season of life are you in, and how does that affect your hopelifting role? Can you offer hope for a season or only for a moment? Finally, look at the needs you can meet. What approach can best meet them? Anonymous, spontaneous, or systematic action? Hope can be expressed in numerous ways, but ultimately we must point each person we encounter to Jesus Himself, the source and giver of all hope.

CHAPTER 12

SPREADING YOUR HOPE

Now He who supplies seed to the sower and bread for food
will also supply and increase your store of seed and will
enlarge the harvest of your righteousness.

—2 CORINTHIANS 9:10

*W*hat do *yellow flowers have to do with being a hopelifter and spreading*
hope? I wondered as I looked at the proposed original cover for this
book.

So I asked God. Ironically, I was at Living Water Retreat Center in Cornville, Arizona, at the time. As I strolled along the creek
I was greeted by an unexpected surprise: an endless row of yellow
wildflowers flanking the creek's bank. In all my years going there I
had never seen them before.

Just then the phrase "spreading like wildflowers" resonated in my
soul. Wildflowers spread contagiously, increasing and expanding,
exactly what hope does. I learned that wild-
flowers spread organically and mysteriously
through the action of wind, bees, and water,
much like hope that can appear in unexpected
ways or places, even in seemingly barren
spots. As Isaiah proclaimed, when "the Spirit
is poured on us from on high ... the desert
becomes a fertile field" (Isaiah 32:15).

> God's kingdom
> spreads as the
> Spirit takes
> His people and
> plants them
> everywhere.

I believe wildflowers represent God's kind
of hope. His kingdom spreads as the Spirit
takes His people and plants them everywhere

113

through a variety of circumstances. I laughed when I thought about wildflowers I've seen growing in unusual places, like sidewalk cracks. If God can bring new life out of the cracks of a sidewalk, how much more life and beauty can He bring through cracked lives?

As my cousin Crystal showed me, God can make beauty out of ashes and extend our hopelifting efforts even beyond our earthly life.

Hidden Hope

"Hey, Cuz."

The familiar sound of Crystal's voice made me smile. She was my favorite cousin, and I always looked up to her. Only a few years older than me, she treated me like a little sister. We'd grown up together in the same small town and sang together in our family's gospel quartet until I moved away after my parents' divorce. Crystal continued to sing and recorded several CDs. Though physical distance kept us apart, Crystal and I stayed close in heart through the years. When my infant son died, Crystal went to a studio and recorded the song "Jesus Has a Rocking Chair" and sent it to comfort me. She continued to call or send funny cards during that dark season of my soul.

Crystal and I talked on the phone regularly and shared our hurts and our dreams. She taught me how to persevere through suffering with a positive attitude. She endured her sister's death to cancer, two failed marriages, physical abuse, the inability to have children, and her dad's Lou Gehrig's disease; yet she never lost her compassion for others, sense of humor, or faith.

"What's up with my favorite cousin?" I asked.

After a few seconds of silence Crystal replied, "I have stage four lung cancer."

I couldn't believe what I was hearing. My mind raced. *This can't be true. Not Crystal. She has never smoked.*

Over the next few minutes, Crystal shared her news and her treatment plan. Her optimism didn't surprise me. Though I don't remember much of that conversation, the words I do remember will forever be etched in my mind. "Kathe, I called you first because I knew you would pray!"

So I did. I cried out to God to lift my cousin and asked Him to be her courage, comforter, strength, and healer. I asked Him to provide close companions to walk this journey with her.

A few days later we talked again. This time she announced, "I'm getting married!"

She and Mac had dated for awhile. Mac's first wife had died. Like Crystal, he'd also endured the painful divorce of a second marriage. Mac and his teenage daughter, Sara, adored Crystal. Even though Mac knew that unless God performed a physical miracle Crystal's time was short, he and Sara talked it over and agreed he and Crystal should get married, and the three of them should become a family for whatever time remained.

Crystal hesitated, not wanting to be a burden, but Mac finally persuaded her to accept his proposal.

As family and friends discovered the devastating news about Crystal, followed by the news of her engagement, they grieved *and* rejoiced. Crystal was loved and admired by the small town where she grew up, and she was even considered a hometown celebrity. The local market sold T-shirts with her picture on it that said "Marquand, Home of Crystal."

What could the town do to encourage her and celebrate her good news in spite of her cancer? A surprise engagement picnic for Crystal and Mac seemed like a perfect idea (or so they thought).

"Shh . . . it's a surprise picnic for Mac and Crystal to celebrate their engagement."

That's what the invitation *said*. However, the truth was, Crystal and Mac were behind the scenes planning this event with a few tight-lipped friends and family so they could bring the town together to celebrate their marriage. "Keep it a secret!" Crystal urged me. What *she* didn't know was *I* was planning to surprise *her* and fly in for this once-in-a-lifetime affair.

With the added strain of chemo, Crystal's dad's declining health, and her mother's worrisome attitude, Crystal decided a surprise wedding was the perfect way to minimize stress. Everyone could show up and enjoy themselves without any fuss over what to wear or buy. The surprise engagement picnic was the way to get everyone in town there. With only two weeks to plan this event, Crystal and her friends decided to keep it simple and low budget. Crystal didn't feel a wedding dress was necessary; however, two friends, Patty and Allison, silently disagreed. They ordered one and surprised Crystal with it two days before the event. To all of their amazement, it fit perfectly. Patty also managed to borrow wedding decorations from another friend's recent wedding reception.

Patty agreed to host the late afternoon event in her lush backyard with its cascading waterfall and swimming pool. Guests arrived at a country paradise of white tents decorated with candles and pink and white ribbons, with the aroma of pulled pork barbeque filling the air. Many from the small town had gathered and were waiting to say "Surprise!" to Crystal and Mac.

Urrrrrrrrrrrrrrrr ... urrrrrRRRRRRR ... URRRRRRR ...

What is that noise? I wondered. I could tell by the questioning stares, others around me were wondering too. "Look, it's Crystal and Mac!" someone shouted and pointed toward red flashing lights. An antique fire engine pulled into the driveway. Crystal and Mac stood on the back bumper dressed in traditional bride and groom attire and waved at the cheering crowd. Mac's profession of selling fire engines enabled him to borrow the antique engine for this memorable grand entrance.

Crystal beamed. She looked beautiful in her flowing white gown, veil, and new wig. A misty-eyed crowd watched the couple stroll down the red brick walkway to the gazebo draped in pink bows and ribbons where they exchanged their marriage vows "... to love and to cherish ... in sickness and in health ... as long as we both shall live, until death we do part."

It was a bittersweet moment for the crowd. Yet, even in the midst of suffering, hope lived, and we rejoiced. A few minutes later, in true Crystal style, she motioned to the band, grabbed the microphone, and started to sing.

Old Friends

Crystal's experimental cancer treatments were not working. With every passing month Crystal weakened. The last time I ever spoke to her was in December 2001, a few months after her wedding. She called to tell me about another event she was planning. "I'm going to sing at my own funeral," she chuckled. With enthusiasm she shared about the program, song choices, and people she had asked to be involved, including her ex-husband, who remained a friend and music partner through the years. She knew her funeral would be an opportunity for many friends and family who did not follow Christ to hear the gospel.

"I'm working on another surprise and hope it gets finished in time," she said.

My curiosity mounted. "What is it?" I asked.

"Old friends," she said. Then she explained how she was recording some of her favorite songs, those she considered "old friends," for her final CD.

I tried hard to hold back the tears, but Crystal could tell by my silence it was a difficult moment for me. "Kathe, can I pray for you?" she asked.

I gratefully received her prayer on the phone that day, then we said, "Good-bye."

That was the last time I ever spoke to Crystal, yet what a fitting way to end our earthly relationship, with the precious sharing of prayer.

A few days later the label cover for Crystal's CD arrived to her home. When Mac showed her, she smiled and sighed, as if to say, "It is finished." Soon after, Crystal died. On December 24, 2001, friends and family gathered again, but this time to celebrate Crystal's home-going to heaven. And in true Crystal style, she sang at her own funeral.

A few weeks later I received her CD in the mail. Hope sings on through her music. I play it often when I miss her, and I'm grateful for this possession that lifts me up.

Hope Sings On

Crystal and I used to joke about going on the road together to tell others about Jesus. "You be the speaker and I'll be the singer," she'd say. Nearly a decade had passed since losing Crystal. One day in 2010, while praying about another bus trip, the thought occurred to me, *Do a snowman bus.*

I started to laugh. Crystal loved snowmen and collected them. I'd given her several through the years. What better way to honor her life than to host a bus trip to take broken-hearted women away for a day with God? So I started planning a holiday-themed bus with Crystal's Christmas CD as the theme music for the day. I was so excited I felt prompted to call Mac, Crystal's husband, to share my news. Although we hadn't spoken in a few years, he welcomed my call and was touched. He told me how he continued to give Crystal's music as a gift and people loved it. He agreed to send me more CDs and surprised me when he offered to help underwrite part of the transportation.

Our "snowman bus" in December of 2010 was memorable for me and a busload of busy women. Together, we journeyed to a country setting to spend a day with God preparing our hearts for Christmas. We sipped hot chocolate out of snowman mugs. We sang Christmas carols and wrapped presents for homeless children. We enjoyed personal time alone with God. I shared Crystal's story of faith and courage and played her music.

Every time I see a snowman, I'm reminded of how God sometimes answers prayers in unexpected ways. Nothing is an obstacle to him, not even death. Crystal and I *did* get to go on the road together and point others to Him. Hope sings on, even after we're gone.

Amazingly, I'm listening to "Old Friends" as I write this and smiling as I imagine Crystal, her sister Debbie, Aunt Wilma and Uncle June, my grandparents, and other family members, including my four green-eyed boys, all gathered in heaven. Perhaps, they are among the great cloud of witnesses cheering me on as I keep writing.

Future Hope

As Crystal's story shows us, hopelifting doesn't have to end after we're gone. Your hope can continue to live on in a multitude of ways. You may spread hope to future generations by providing a place like a cabin, camping spot, or Christian school, or through your support of a retreat center or ministry that provides a place for hurting people to be refreshed.

One woman is working on spreading future hope through a possession, a personal Bible for each of her children and grandchildren. Selecting a unique version or style to fit every family member, she is reading through each Bible and making personal notes or highlighting passages so after she's gone God's words (and hers) live on.

> *You may spread hope to future generations.*

My mom has a red-sequined prayer box that we open when I visit her, and we pray for our family and future generations. Although it looks empty to the human eye, the unseen Scriptures prayed and requests held within it will be answered in God's timing. We've already seen many miracles in our family. In time, this prayer box will be passed on to me and to others in our family who will spread hope through prayer.

Mom also crocheted me a prayer shawl—"every stitch with praise, thanksgiving, and Scripture prayers for me," she says. It's her way of staying close in heart though distance separates us, and spreading hope to me in a tangible and intangible way. I keep it on my nightstand. Many times when I've felt anxious in the middle of the night, I've grabbed it and God has used it to bring me peace. The power of prayer knows no boundaries and lasts forever.

Hope sings on when you invest in others who work together and make spreading God's hope a practice—churches, ministries, organizations, mission organizations, Christian schools, or missionary training centers. Many years ago, my husband, Rich, and I felt prompted to support Marty, the leader of our young couples class at church. Marty loved helping teenagers find worth and meaning in Jesus Christ. By practicing the ministry of presence through weekly clubs, crazy games, and camps, he showed God's love and was the hands and feet of Jesus. At that time in the early 1980s he was raising his financial support to serve in our city. We joyfully became supporters. Amazingly, that investment produced more than we ever imagined it would. Today, our former Sunday school teacher is one of the key international leaders of Young Life, a dynamic ministry to young people, influencing multitudes for Jesus Christ.

Investing in the person of Jesus, the chief Hopelifter, is an investment that continues to spread hope.

Ultimately, investing in the person of Jesus, the chief Hopelifter, is an investment that continues to spread and give hope. Someday, he'll return as the bridegroom to take us as his bride to celebrate an eternal wedding. The eternal wedding is coming sooner than you think, and many still need to be invited and RSVP.

I don't want to be surprised by who's not in heaven because of opportunities I've missed to invite them. I want everyone I know to be there too, celebrating and experiencing hope to the full in God's forever presence. I'll finally have the opportunity to thank the multitudes of hopelifters who have spread hope to me and made a difference in my life. What a party it will be!

Keep spreading hope to hurting people, dear friend and fellow hopelifter. A multitude of hopelifters are waiting to cheer you on and offer support and creative ideas. Next in this book are their Recipes of Hope to help you spread hope to others. When you trust God and offer yourself and your resources wholeheartedly, He will surprise you by magnifying your efforts and spreading hope beyond what you can see, even beyond the grave. Like wildflowers scattered on a riverbank, may the beauty of his hope spread and become contagious!

See you at the wedding! I'll introduce you to Crystal. I'm sure she'll be singing.

PART THREE

GIVING HOPE

CHAPTER 13

ONE HUNDRED RECIPES OF HOPE

Why, my soul, are you downcast?
Why so disturbed within me?
Put your hope in God,
*   for I will yet praise Him,*
*   my Savior and my God.*

—PSALM 42:5, 11; 43:5

The following section contains what I call "Recipes of Hope," stories of people who have found hope and help even in the midst of their suffering. Each story is labeled with a life issue that requires hopelifting; issues as public and widespread as bereavement, and issues as private and painful as abortion or rejection. I include these stories because each one contains within it creative ideas I call "Recipes of Hope"—ways that people have been encouraged (or have themselves done the encouraging) that brought comfort to them in dark times.

Similar to a cookbook, these "Recipes of Hope" will inspire you and guide you in collecting the ingredients to prepare meaningful hope for those who are hurting. Written in their own words by fellow hopelifters who have experienced the life issue or have helped someone who has, the recipes are practical, thoughtful, and creative, and will help you to become the hands and feet of Jesus to someone who is hurting.

Unlike a cookbook, however, you cannot follow these "recipes" exactly and expect to have the same result. In fact, I would advise you *not* to. In every situation where you are offering hope, you must respond to what the Holy Spirit is calling you to do or you risk causing more hurt than help. When in doubt, ask a fellow believer what might be appropriate in that situation, or keep your response low-key, offering a listening ear or practical help until you know more. And don't always expect to know more. The hurting person may take only a few people into their confidence, so adjust your help to what you are able to offer and what they seem willing to receive from you.

Although the recipes of hope are arranged alphabetically by topic, hopelifting actions in one scenario often apply to many other scenarios as well. Practical help is almost always needed in crisis situations, and so is a listening ear. Cards and appropriate words of caring support are always welcome. And prayer, of course, is the main ingredient for any recipe of hope. You may not know people suffering from all the categories listed here, but each of the stories will remind you that hurts and hope come in many different forms, and the creativity of the Spirit in spreading hope to hurting people is unlimited! So read the recipes for inspiration, but make each recipe your own, seasoned with your gifts, personality, and the Spirit's sensitivity to the situation.

You might also choose to use these "Recipes of Hope" to guide you in prayer. Choose a topic and pray for that specific category of people who are hurting, or reach out to someone in that situation in a tangible way. Some of the stories may even open your eyes to hurts you had never before encountered. That's another reason for these stories: to let you know there is a world of needs out there, and a world of ways to creatively address them!

In some cases, you will find that the recipe's category applies to yourself or the recipes are designed to be followed by the one who is suffering. Hopelifters, of course, are not exempt from suffering and trials. So the recipes at times will include hints and tips for self-care. Jesus said, "Love your neighbor as yourself" (Matthew 22:39). So if you are in a time of trial, remember to treat yourself with the same kindness and compassion as you extend to others at those times.

At the end of the "Recipes of Hope" are lined blank pages for you to write your own recipes. You can find more "Recipes of Hope" at www.hopelifters.com.

THE TRUTH SETS YOU FREE

Gia Chapman (told to Kathe Wunnenberg)

MY FRIEND GIA, A MOTHER OF FIVE LIVING CHILDREN AND FOUR babies in heaven, recalled the following personal story of her first child.

What will others think if they know I am pregnant? wondered twenty-year-old Gia.

Her perfect little Christian-girl-next-door image would be shattered. To make matters worse, she and her boyfriend had parted ways. Alone, unmarried, and afraid, she decided to keep her secret to herself and not tell her parents.

Instead, Gia sought counsel from a friend. She discovered one visit to a clinic would solve her problem and save her reputation. Both the friend and clinic said she'd be having "a termination" before anything was formed in the pregnancy. Gia listened to their lies.

No one has to know, she rationalized. Yet something deep within her whispered that what she was considering was wrong. She went to the clinic anyway. Ironically, a very pregnant nurse was assigned to her. Still, she continued, it was a horrific experience. For the next four years, she lived with private guilt and shame and masked her pain in an eating disorder.

Finally, she sought help through a post-abortive Bible study. She faced the truth that she needed to forgive herself. If she didn't, it was as if she was slapping the Lord in the face and saying He wasn't good enough for her personal sin. He covered *all* sin, even her terrible choice of abortion.

She also sought forgiveness from those affected by her choice. She found comfort in knowing she would someday meet her baby, Colby, in heaven.

If you know someone who is suffering from her decision to have an abortion, put her in touch with a crisis pregnancy center, where she can find resources such as post-abortion counseling and support groups. Encourage her to name her baby, and remember to pray for her on Mother's Day.

GLIMMERS OF HOPE IN THE CONGO

Karen Lynn Ray

MY HUSBAND AND I RECENTLY RETURNED FROM A LIFE-CHANGING medical mission trip to the Democratic Republic of Congo. We had a limited idea of the horrific abuses and poverty suffered by the vulnerable people in this war-ravaged country

Nevertheless, we armed ourselves with duffle bags stuffed with antibiotics, antifungal crème, and an assortment of additional medical supplies. My husband, the physician, was prepared to treat the precious orphans of Eastern Congo. And I, the counselor, was prepared to share a word of hope to the hurting Congolese women.

I was in for a big surprise! I heard many, many stories of pain and heartache. Yet, in the midst of unimaginable abuse and oppression, I saw glimmers of hope sprinkled throughout the painful memories. For those who called upon the name of the Lord, God's truth was evident through their stories: *nothing* could separate them from God's love. Their true identity, worth, and value was in him. God whispered to me, "Can you see that I am here? I understand this pain and I care." Like Jesus, who saw beyond the woman at the well's circumstance to her thirst for Living Water and true identity in Him, God opened my eyes to know and see the truth of who these women were in him: beautiful and loved.

When preparing to offer hope to someone in difficult circumstances, first pray and ready your heart by embracing *your* true identity in who God says you are. (Read Psalm 119.) Next, invite the Holy Spirit to open your heart to hear and see others' hurts. Listen well. Look deeper than their circumstances to the person beyond the pain. Point them to Jesus, the Living Water, and their identity in Him and His Word. Don't be surprised when God gives you glimmers of His hope and waters your soul through theirs.

MANAGING THE MINEFIELD

Karen Howells

IT'S THE LAST THING ANY PARENT EXPECTS, AND I'VE LEARNED SINCE it happened to my son that addiction is truly no respecter of persons. People and their families at all levels of income, education, faiths, and backgrounds suffer from addiction, and it's on the rise. Illegal and abusive prescription drug use was up 400 percent in the year 2011. It's beyond alarming as a social trend and totally devastating when it's your beloved child.

My son became addicted to what was initially a legally prescribed substance to help treat symptoms of his cystic fibrosis. Today, he is clean, sober, and doing extremely well. He's living on his own, has a part-time job, and just received his first belt in martial arts.

But recovery is a long road. After all the heartbreaking realities of being a mother of a recovering opiate and heroin addict, we've managed to emerge through the minefields and have a good relationship with him.

Lessons I've learned on this journey of helping someone with an addiction problem:

- *Get professional help* as soon as you have a tiny inkling there's a problem.
- *Be supportive in their recovery*, but don't try to be "the savior." Groups like Celebrate Recovery and Al-Anon will help you make sure you don't fall into codependent or enabling patterns of behavior, and they will provide much-needed support to *you*. Because you will need support for yourself and lots of it. If you're married, don't bear it alone. It's too heavy and can crush your marriage. Get support from a professional counselor, your church leaders, and trusted friends.
- *Stay connected.* Even at the lowest point of his addiction when our son was actually on the streets, had stolen from us, and repeatedly lied, we stayed in communication with him.
- *Expect relapse.* It's a part of recovery. People do get clean and sober, but it takes time.
- *Cry out to God.* I spent many hours walking on the junior high school track nearby shouting out my anguish.

SUPPORTING THE FAMILY OF AN ADDICT

Donna Morris

WHAT WOULD THE WORLD BE LIKE WITHOUT ADDICTIONS OR addicts? I have often asked myself this question and tried to envision the implications to my world. Addictions change the life of an addict; that is a given. But loving someone who happens to have an addiction is also life changing. Many of my friends' grown children and my family members struggle with addictions.

I once aided a friend who had less than twenty-four hours to get her son into a drug rehabilitation facility. I conducted research on various programs to learn what types of services were available, and then conveyed the information back to her. My friend, on the other hand, was left with the reality of making the choice of which program would best help him. In the end, she flew him to one of the facilities for what was supposed to be an eighteen-month program. Unfortunately, he checked himself out from the program after only six months and relapsed shortly thereafter.

In this situation, I was needed to provide practical support by researching rehabilitation programs, but I also listened to my friend, provided moral support, and prayed for her and her son.

Every person is different; therefore, the type of encouragement that should be offered to a person who loves someone with an addiction should vary, too. Encourage them to take care of themselves first and foremost. Provide creative solutions, as many times the loved one cannot think past their own pain. Pray for them and let them know often you are thinking about them and their loved one. And make sure they are receiving professional counseling or lay counseling through Stephens Ministries or attending a support group such as Celebrate Recovery.

ADOPTION

WELCOME HOME CELEBRATION

Kathe Wunnenberg

I'LL NEVER FORGET THE DAY WE PICKED JAKE UP FROM THE ADOPTION agency. Twenty of our closest friends huddled together in the downstairs lobby with balloons. Hand in hand, Rich and I ascended the spiral staircase with diaper bag in tow and entered the room at the top. My heart was racing as I walked toward a couple holding a ten-pound, alert baby boy. I immediately noticed Jake's large brown eyes. Our eyes locked as I walked toward him and the transition mom placed Jake in my arms. *Finally, I'm a mom.* I thought. Although Jake didn't grow *under* my heart, through God's power, he would grow *in* it. Handpicked by God and his birthmother, I would be Jake's spiritual mom and lifelong intercessor. My role was irrevocable.

Moments later we introduced our son to a cheering, applauding crowd of friends and enjoyed a time of refreshments and group pictures with our new baby.

When we arrived home, our garage door sported this sign from our neighbors: "It's a Boy! Welcome Home, Jake!"

The welcome-home celebration continued with meals, flower deliveries, phone calls, and visits from friends. During the following two weeks, three baby showers were held to welcome our new son. Among my favorite gifts received were a rocking chair and a Shower of Blessing—when friends read a chosen Bible verse as a prayer for Jake. If you know someone who has adopted a child, welcome him to your neighborhood, church, or family with joy and celebrations!

JET LAGGED AND EXHAUSTED

Louise Nichols

FINALLY WE WERE HOME. AFTER TWENTY-EIGHT HOURS OF TRAVEL from Guangzhou, China, I was exhausted. I wearily led Kate, my precious newly adopted four-year-old daughter, into our home. Feeling overwhelmed, I doubted I could do this "single mom" thing. I felt myself wanting to cry. The lump in my throat grew larger until the tears spilled out. And spill they did for the next two days. At night, I sat before the Lord and wept. It was my mom, my hope-lifter, who reminded me I was not falling apart emotionally. I was simply jet-lagged. My mom also went grocery shopping for me the day before we came home. There was food galore! What a blessing it was.

I love 2 Corinthians 1:3–4, which says, "Praise be to the God and Father of our Lord Jesus Christ, the Father of compassion and the God of all comfort, who comforts us in all our troubles, so that we can comfort those in any trouble with the comfort we ourselves receive from God."

Over the years, I've been able to offer comfort and hope to other moms as they return home from traveling to adopt their children. I have assured many, "It's just jet lag." I have delivered many meals and provided rides from the airport. It brings me great pleasure to walk alongside other adoptive moms who are feeling as I once did. My favorite moments are watching 2 Corinthians 1:3–4 lived out in their own lives as they, too, comfort young adoptive mothers.

If you know someone who is adopting from overseas, offer a listening ear and kind words of encouragement. Bring over a meal or a gift card to a restaurant. Offer to go grocery shopping, or bring over a bag full of basic groceries, like milk, bread, eggs, and so on. And above all, celebrate the adoption with the new family!

RECTANGULAR SWORDS

Erica Wiggenhorn

"I'M HAVING AN AFFAIR WITH MY BOSS."

My friend's confession slapped me in the face like an icy snowball. *How could this be?* This was my best friend, an amazing woman of God who had walked with her husband faithfully for so long. Questions flooded my mind.

Finally I sputtered, "Well, what are you going to do?"

She crumbled in a heap on her sofa and sobbed, "I need your help!"

I knew she needed accountability; she would face daily temptation. Quitting her job simply wasn't an option. How would she walk through this in victory?

Then my phone rang. An idea immediately sprang to mind. This phone would become my rectangular sword. I would use it to help slay her dragon. Every hour I'd text her a verse and she'd respond—a reminder she had a sister in Christ, standing beside her in battle.

"Take up the shield of faith, with which you can extinguish all the flaming arrows of the evil one" (Ephesians 6:16). The truth of God's Word would protect her mind and put out the fire of temptation. I looked up verses about God's love for her, about God being her husband, and about His strength. And I texted my thumbs off! Eventually my friend ended the affair and strengthened her relationship with her husband.

If you discover someone you know is having an affair, first pray and ask God for wisdom. If she's not a believer, demonstrate unconditional love and concern through a listening ear or timely help that reveals her need for Jesus. If she is a believer, share privately (Matthew 18:15a) about her need to change and be willing to help her overcome temptation by offering your time, ideas, people, or resources. Restored fellowship with God is your goal. If she refuses to change, pray for courage to gather others to help (Matthew 18:15b).

MONDAYS WITH MOM

Mary Jane Farr

OUR FAMILY HAS ALWAYS BEEN CLOSE, BUT MOM WAS THE ONE WHO encouraged and supported me the most. Something seemed missing when our daily call was overlooked. While praying for Mom, I sensed from God that I should try to spend at least one day a month taking her shopping or just hanging out with her.

Mom seldom complained about anything, especially her health. However, she gradually found her daily mile walk with her faithful dog Shadow difficult. At eighty years of age, she had open-heart surgery, replacing a heart valve. Her surgery was a success, but her kidneys failed, and she was placed on dialysis three days a week. My siblings and I each had a day with Mom, and my day was Monday!

God answered my prayer, but instead of just one day a month, I was blessed to spend one day a week with Mom, taking her to dialysis and grocery shopping, and then sharing an evening centered on games, laughter, and dinner. Even though I thought I was serving her and encouraging her, she taught me life is precious just being together and there's no amount of money to compensate for that time.

Mom knew her Bible, prayed often, and modeled Christlikeness. We did not quote verses to each other; we just lived life together, and at the end of her life there were no regrets. I got to say good-bye knowing one day I would see her again. It was on a Monday that Mom went to heaven!

As you look for ways to engage aging parents, be open to God's leading. Step out in faith. Celebrate life. And choose the joy of togetherness. If distance separates you, make "phone dates" or send cards or flowers. Find ways to show your respect and love in their last years of life.

SUPPORT TEAM

Kathe Wunnenberg

LATE ONE EVENING I CALLED MY MOM AND DISCOVERED SHE WAS extremely ill and couldn't walk to her bedroom. *What can I do from 1,500 miles away?* I wondered. *God help!* I prayed. Immediately, I called my brother who lives nearby, and we brainstormed possible solutions. We agreed I should call Mom's friend Patricia and enlist her to help for the night. When I called Mom with this idea, she seemed relieved. Within thirty minutes Patricia arrived and became the hands and feet of Jesus to my mom (and me) for the night.

Supporting your aging parents nearby or from afar can be challenging at times. Being proactive to develop a strategy of support for them can help ease your mind and theirs when a need arises. First, assess their needs. What physical needs do they have? Do they need help with household chores, shopping, or cooking? What emotional needs do they have? Is companionship or conversation important? I call both of my parents most days and purchased a computer for my mom to provide an opportunity for her to connect with others. How are their spiritual needs being met? If your parents can't attend church, bring church to them through a podcast, TV broadcast, or DVD series.

Next, determine what resources are available. The Area Agency on Aging is a great place to start. Who are the people resources available, and where could you look to find them (church, medical, friends, family, neighbors, school, insurance company)? Who could you ask to help?

Last, and most important, enlist a PIT Team (Personal Intercessory Team) for your parents. Perhaps you and a few others who also have aging parents could agree to support one another by praying for one another's parents.

DEALING WITH DERMATOMYOSITIS

Adrienne Schiele

GOD ALWAYS FIRST TRIES TO GET MY ATTENTION IN SMALL WAYS, and He subtly keeps talking to me when I fail to heed that still, small voice inside my heart. Finally, He ends up having to scream at me to get my attention.

That voice started out small with weakness, a rash, tiredness, and trouble swallowing. I couldn't be convinced something was really wrong until the voice screamed at me when the rash spread to my face. God now had my full attention.

I was sent for a battery of tests and referred to three different specialists. The diagnosis was dermatomyositis, an autoimmune disease that is a cousin to lupus. I was afraid, but I remembered that Jesus promised us, "Surely I am with you always, to the very end of the age" (Matthew 28:20). I knew He would be next to me through every appointment, every test, and every treatment.

It has been two years since I first started on this journey. God has kept His promise to be with me every step of the way. The appointments and tests are fewer and farther apart now. The medication dose has been lowered, and God has not left my side.

I may not totally shed this illness until my death, or I may have a remission very soon. Only God knows the answer to that question.

John 16:33 says, "In this world you will have trouble. But take heart! I have overcome the world." When you are given something unexpected and unwelcome, remember this recipe for perseverance:

- Listen to God's voice.
- Be obedient and focus on what you can do, not on what you can't.
- Leave what you can't do in God's hands.

LOVING ONE ANOTHER WELL

Kathe Wunnenberg

"'Love the Lord your God with all your heart and with all your soul and with all your mind.' This is the first and greatest commandment. And the second is like it: 'Love your neighbor as yourself'" (Matthew 22:37–39).

When Bethany Christian School in Tempe, Arizona, announced this theme verse for 2011–2012, they had no idea their school community would experience the death of a student, a teacher, and two moms that year, requiring them to live the verse more intentionally. Their board, staff, students, and families became the hands and feet of Jesus to one another during an extreme year of sorrow.

BCS was prepared to respond, and just needed a plan. The staff cried out to God for help in each unique situation. God's creative compassion flowed through their brainstorming, resulting in a variety of planned activities and spontaneous acts that allowed the school community to express their grief and to love one another in meaningful ways.

Making posters, a student memorial service, prayer circles, grief education, a farewell video, a heart-to-heart room for prayer and conversation, wearing "green" to honor the lost student, making commemorative t-shirts, creating a scrapbook, and meal deliveries were a few of the ideas God gave them.

The outpouring of hope and love through simple acts of kindness, like handing someone a tissue, speaking a timely word, giving a hug, and kids praying with other kids, was seen often on the campus.

The Moms in Prayer group decided to adopt "in prayer" the students who lost their moms. Standing in the gap for the moms now in heaven, they cried out to God for the hearts of the children left behind.

By the end of the year, hope lived again. The school community could say with confidence, "We loved God and one another well."

How do you survive loss or tragedy at your school, church, workplace, or community? Cry out to God. Ask Him to give you creative compassion. Cry out to people. Gather a few people to brainstorm. Determine needs. Share the needs with others. Then simply cry out. Embrace sorrow and embrace each other in mutual grief and support.

THE UPSIDE OF DOWN

Starr Ayers

HIS WORDS WERE UNNECESSARY. HIS BODY LANGUAGE REVEALED ALL I wanted to know.

Pink bows, rosebud bouquets, and bubble-gum cigars could not silence the incessant replay of our physician's words inside my head, nor dismiss the unwelcome companion they heralded.

"Your baby has Down syndrome!"

Our precious daughter's birth: a joyous event now filled with crushing pain and an avalanche of contradictory emotions and prayers. Prayers thanking God the disability was not more severe, and yet prayers asking for miracles that would change the diagnosis, miracles that would somehow make everything different.

Was this really God's answer for our family?

Only the passing of time would reveal God's astounding ability to take a situation often perceived as tragic and transform it into a beautiful gift that would change our lives. Within this tiny parcel wrapped in pink came a contagious love, tied with our growing awareness of God's unshakable presence and His overwhelming desire for us to know Him and experience His ways. "And we know that in all things God works for the good of those who love Him, who have been called according to His purpose" (Romans 8:28).

Yes, in *all* things! Even the birth of a special needs child is a "special delivery" indeed. If you know someone who has given birth to a special needs child, remember these four Ps.

Pray. Ask God to help you reach out appropriately to the family.

Presence. Visit the family. Exhibit a spirit of unconditional acceptance.

Praise. Ooh and aah! Every mom needs to know her baby is beautiful and valued.

Presents. Gifts for mom or the baby are always welcome, including meals, gift certificates, or baby clothes and accessories.

A BAG OF ORANGES

Linda Grabeman

CANCER. IT'S A DIFFICULT JOURNEY. BUT GOD HAS ALWAYS BEEN ready and willing to provide for His people in need. Even better, He loves to engage other Christians to bring that provision. He calls each of us at times to lift up discouraged and despairing hearts. By His power in us, He can transform even a tough road like cancer into an unexpected blessing.

What if we ask God to open our eyes to the wonderful ways we could be a hopelifter to our cancer-plodding friends? We must then make sure we follow His leading. My dear friend Libby learned that lesson the hard way. While she was praying for me, the Lord impressed the word *oranges* on her heart. She allowed someone to pooh-pooh that idea. Later that day she wailed loud and long when I told how I would have gladly paid one hundred dollars for just one orange after my chemotherapy! From then on she brought me bags of oranges. Those bites of juicy, citrus fruit were not life-changing for me, but they were certainly life-enhancing. They calmed my queasy tummy, put a smile on my face, and made me feel loved.

So send cards, emails, phone messages, flowers, or food. But also remember how creative our God is. Be willing to think outside the box if He leads you there. My friend Carolyn left me a perfectly smooth, oval stone at my front doorstep. It bore just one word, lovingly written in Sharpie: COURAGE. It now sits on my kitchen ledge to remind me of her love and God's provision.

In God's hands, an offering as small as an orange or a smooth stone can be supernaturally used to bring healing and love far surpassing anything you could ever imagine!

TANGIBLE TOKENS OF LOVE

Tanya Glanzman

WHEN MY THIRTEEN-YEAR-OLD DAUGHTER WAS DIAGNOSED WITH lymphoma, my family's entire world was turned upside down. Within hours, a typical pediatrician's visit turned into a six-day stay in the pediatric intensive care unit. Doctors worked to ensure that the tumor, filling her entire chest cavity and placing pressure on both her heart and trachea, was not cutting off her air supply. We were thrown into crisis mode, yet the practical aspects of everyday life remained.

The release of our daughter from the hospital was only the beginning of the journey. Chemotherapy treatments, scans, spinal taps, and emergency room visits when her temperature reached 100.4 or higher all became our new normal.

At this time it was the practical in tangible form that ministered most to our family. We needed childcare for our other child, and someone to take care of our dog and our yard. We needed someone to act as a contact person to give updates to family and friends. We appreciated home-cooked meals brought to the hospital in disposable containers. Some offered meals through gift cards or cash. Once our daughter was home from the hospital, we appreciated prepared meals in disposable containers on chemotherapy days, as well as special attention given to our other child on those days. Simple acts by those who ran errands or shopped for groceries made a big difference in our lives. And we needed our closest friends and family to simply listen, cry, pray, and just sit with us. Not everyone can do everything. But many hands chipped in to help us in many different ways, and we appreciated them all.

PRACTICAL, PRICELESS HOPE

Lisa Kowalski

I AM CONTINUOUSLY IN AWE OF HOW THE GREAT HOPELIFTER USES all my life experiences to train me for His hopelifter missions — each designed to grow me into a woman He can use, including our son's cancer.

With great care, the Lord allowed this unwanted guest to arrive during a season filled with family, thankfulness, and distraction: Thanksgiving. In the blink of an eye, we were shoved into a foreign world of new terminology, complicated medical procedures, and total strangers appointed to save our son.

The rapidly progressing disease demanded organization. So I grabbed the nearest black binder and started filing. As the cancer battle raged on, this simple binder became our memory, recalling details when we were too confused or too exhausted to remember. Like an efficient assistant, it provided order so we could focus on the bigger picture. Little did I realize God was supplying a shiny new tool for my hopelifter toolbox.

When healing came it was bye, bye black binder! Had I forgotten my earlier prayer asking the Lord to use our suffering for His glory?

A year later, the news of my girlfriend's cancer pushed me right back through that hefty cancer door. I thought, *She needs a practical, yet cute cancer binder!* Before long, I was mailing practical hope to folks in and out of state. So simple to do, yet a mammoth of a blessing!

Here's how to turn a simple three-ring binder into a symbol of hope and a tool for help:

- Use craft supplies to create a personalized binder cover.
- Fill the binder with sheet protectors (to collect brochures and information) and index tab dividers specific to the cancer. Categories could include: staging, oncologist, surgery, labs, imaging, chemotherapy, radiation, medications, and hospitalization. If you are unsure which categories to include, leave the dividers blank for the patient to fill in as needed.
- Finally and most importantly, always cover the binder with prayer.

❧ CANCER ❧

LONG-DISTANCE LOVE

Kathe Wunnenberg

WHEN MY AUNT PAT WAS DIAGNOSED WITH CANCER, 1,500 MILES separated us. "God, please show me how I can be close in heart and encourage her!" I prayed. I expected an immediate reply from God; instead, my stomach gurgled. Rationalizing I would be able to think clearer on a full stomach, I drove to a nearby restaurant known for "down home" cooking. When I walked inside, three life-sized stuffed angels greeted me with permanent smiles. I chuckled as I dined on dumplings and recalled my first job as a waitress working with Aunt Pat. My amazement mounted as I suddenly remembered we both collected angels.

With confidence, I knew God had answered my prayer and I left with "Faith," "Hope," and "Love," my three new nicknamed angels. I raced to the post office and stuffed "Love" into a box with this note:

> *Aunt Pat,*
>   *Since I can't be there with you, I've sent "Love" instead. Every time you look at her know that God loves you and I love you, too, and am praying for you. She'll be your companion since I can't be. Enjoy!*
>

Love,
Kathe
>

During the following weeks I heard about Love's adventures. She accompanied Aunt Pat to chemo, hid in the bathroom to surprise visitors, and brought humor and companionship when I couldn't. She even attended Aunt Pat's memorial.

A few weeks later, a box arrived at my doorstep. I opened it and Love stared back at me with her silly smile (one of Aunt Pat's final requests ... to mail her back to me). God's love never fails, and when you give love away, it *always* comes back to you!

If you want to support someone who lives far away, pray and ponder over what gift might best bring joy to their heart. And look for God's answer!

PIZZA PARTY

Kathe Wunnenberg

AUNT JANE'S HEALTH WAS DECLINING. MY COUSIN SHERRY, HER only child, was weary from long days and nights at the hospital and from being her primary caregiver. Sherry rarely got a break.

One day Sherry called to tell me Aunt Jane's condition was getting worse. She sounded depressed. As always, I listened and prayed with her on the phone. I longed to do more. I lived two hours away and had young children, so driving there that day was not an option.

Who do I know that could stop by and see Sherry? I wondered. Unfortunately, no names came to mind. Since Sherry was unable to attend church, she didn't have a pastor or church family.

God, how can I give her hope? I prayed.

Then I had the idea to deliver hope to her. My mind reeled with possibilities: a gift from the hospital gift shop, flowers, or food from the cafeteria. None of the options seemed right.

Have a pizza delivered.

This thought excited me. At that moment, I saw a pizza commercial on television. I called them and explained the situation and asked, "Can you deliver a pizza to the hospital?"

When they agreed, I was ecstatic. At that time, payment couldn't be made over the phone or online. I told them I would be in town later that week and would stop by and pay them. To my surprise, they agreed to these terms.

Later that evening, I received an enthusiastic call from my cousin. Apparently, the anonymous pizza had arrived to the nurses' station and they summoned my cousin from her mother's room. Together, they all celebrated and had a pizza party.

If you know someone going through an extended hospitalization or illness, think not only of the patient but also of their caregivers' needs. How can you care for the caregivers? Perhaps a pepperoni pizza is just what the Holy Spirit would order!

UNEXPECTED CELEBRATION

Charity Worden

BY THE TIME WE KNEW MOM'S BREAST CANCER HAD RETURNED, IT had advanced to the point that no treatment would conquer it. We began our all-too-brief process of good-byes and braced ourselves for an unknown journey with a well-known conclusion. My family and I were already living with her, and I felt blessed that God had orchestrated our lives so I could care for her. She would be home where she wanted to be, and we would collect a few more invaluable memories. It was an intense, beautiful time, but it was taxing.

Under those circumstances, sometimes it's the insignificant things that tip the sanity scale. One week, my ever-increasing crop of grey hair was getting the best of me, so I called Corie the Cosmetologist to the rescue. Somehow, someone got the inside scoop about where I'd be. Walking into the salon, I was greeted by a table loaded with goodies, flanked by a few triumphantly grinning ladies from my church. I stopped, confused, trying to make out what I had missed. "Surprise! It's 'Celebrate Charity Day'!" With the spark of an idea and a few phone calls, they had created an opportunity to celebrate ... me! I was speechless.

For the next three hours, we chatted and snacked while Corie worked her wonders. Other customers wandered in and out, taking our infectious giggling with them. There were no speeches, no condolences. None were needed. They were there to be *with* me: love simply expressed through presence. I left with my hair and my heart a whole lot lighter. My heart is still wearing its new look.

Do you know someone who is in an intense season of caregiving? Look for opportunities to lift their spirits with your presence, humor, pampering, or other tokens of support.

WALK BY FAITH

Sharon Cochran

IT WAS THE HOMECOMING FOOTBALL GAME OF MY SEVENTEEN-YEAR-old son, Dillon. We were looking forward to this memorable event, watching him play. But in the third quarter of the game, Dillon was hit hard.

"You need to come. Dillon's been hurt!"

My husband's words didn't alarm me. I thought Dillon had broken an arm or busted his chin. I was unprepared to see him lying unconscious, convulsing. Immediately, I knelt down and prayed. Minutes later, in the ambulance, I called Katherine, my missionary friend, and Victoria, who had lost a child. I asked them to pray too.

At the hospital we were informed that Dillon needed brain surgery. A craniotomy would be done, and he might not survive. I wept in my husband's arms and cried out to God, "Please don't take him tonight!"

I felt the Lord carrying me through the darkest hours of my life. At that moment, I decided to live by faith and not by sight.

Others carried me too. Teammates, coaches, students, and school staff gathered in the waiting room. I was amazed when the football coach of a rival school showed up and announced he was the director of ICU and would be observing Dillon's surgery and giving us updates. Only God could have orchestrated this.

Finally, after several hours, we got word that the surgery went well, though the next seventy-two hours were critical. Moreover, he would probably be paralyzed and blind on one side.

Multitudes prayed. Calls, texts, and visitors helped me walk in faith. One person dropped off a snack basket with a journal, which I used to record miracle events, including Dillon's waking up, eating his first meal, and leaving the hospital eighteen days later.

Prayer and Scripture is the best medicine for those who are going through a crisis. Read Psalm 57:1–5; Psalm 138; Jeremiah 1:8; 2 Corinthians 5:7. Help them walk by faith, not by sight.

CHEMO COUNTDOWN CHAIN

Janet Drez

ONE HUNDRED EIGHTY DAYS OF CHEMOTHERAPY. SIX LONG MONTHS of daily hospital visits, IVs, nausea, and hair loss. That was the aggressive treatment course my sweet friend Linda was about to embark upon to hopefully rid her body of uterine cancer.

What could I do to make this time less daunting and more encouraging? Recalling my children's "countdown to Christmas" paper chains, I set to work and started typing: a Bible verse, a personal memory, a hilarious knock-knock joke, or an inspirational quote for each day. I recruited our mutual girlfriends to add their notes, favorite verses, and riddles until we had exactly 180 links for the chain. I typed them up, signed the writer's names, printed them on bright colored paper, and then cut them into strips and taped them together in a long chain.

When I arrived at Linda's home on the first day of her treatment, I explained what the chain was and how to use it. "Right now this chain looks long and a little intimidating, but day by day as you pull the links off the chain, you'll know you are making progress and you'll know you are loved and prayed for."

Over the next six months Linda's chain became part of her family room décor. Each day Linda and her family would anticipate pulling another link off the chain to see what encouragement would be found there. Many times during those months Linda called me to tell me how a message on a specific day was just what the doctor ordered.

If you know someone going through chemo, look for creative ways to encourage them over the long haul. And never stop praying!

LISTEN TO LIFE

Kathe Wunnenberg

WHEN I HEARD MY COUSIN WAS IN A COMA A FEW STATES AWAY, I knew exactly what to do.

My friend Margie Erbe had experienced being in a coma and wasn't expected to live, but she miraculously recovered. I remember hearing her share her story from her book, *My Joy Came in the Morning*. She said she could hear people praying, and that encouraged her while she was unconscious. Her story motivated me to reach out to my cousin's family.

"I'm mailing you the dramatized Bible on tape," I announced.

I told them Margie's story and asked for their help. They agreed to bring a tape player to the hospital and play it 'round the clock. For several days my cousin listened to God's life-giving words as he lay in limbo between consciousness and death. Finally, he woke up and started his journey of recovery.

Although I'm not sure my cousin had a personal relationship with God before his coma, I do know he had the opportunity to hear the truth and to choose life by listening to God's Word while in his coma.

People say that the last sense to depart before death is hearing, so even if someone in a coma is expected to pass away, they too need the comforting words of Scripture spoken over them. Read familiar passages from the Psalms, John 14, 1 Corinthians 13, or John's vision of heaven in Revelation 21. Sing or play hymns or songs. Minister through the ear. When someone is in a coma or dying, it's a wonderful opportunity to spread hope through God's Word.

WHAT A DYING PERSON NEEDS: "APPLES"

Diane Meehl

MY MOTHER IS DYING FROM CANCER. SCRATCH THAT: SHE'S *LIVING* with cancer. She's quick to point it out; she's still here. And while cancer is winning the battle, my mother claims victory. The spoils?

"Apples." But not McIntosh or Fuji. Let me explain.

It's not easy to find the right words to say to a person nearing the end of life. But words—spoken, written down, or prayed—shoulder the power to heal, comfort, and connect. Proverbs 25:11 (1984) illustrates so eloquently: "A word aptly spoken is like apples of gold in settings of silver."

During her journey, my mother has received countless "apples." Those eternal gifts were "aptly spoken" via cards, prayers, and conversations, each word a sweet balm.

People often struggle to express what a dying person longs to hear. What can we say to reverse the ravages of chemotherapy? What mere words could convey our sorrow? How do we express our fear and give voice to theirs?

My answer is this: embrace vulnerability and find creative ways to deliver those "apples of gold." Here's how:

- *Read the Bible aloud.* God's Word offers comfort you sometimes cannot articulate. Try Psalm 23 for starters.
- *Write a letter.* Don't hold back; it might be easier to pen your feelings rather than speak them.
- *Use humor.* Many cancer patients want to feel normal. My mother's best friend often looked at my mom in all her bald-headed glory and said, "Well, Karen, we're going to get out of your *hair* now."
- *Say good-bye.* This is perhaps the scariest part. I simply held my mother's hand and told her that despite our difficult seasons, I loved her.

WHAT DYING PEOPLE NEED

Judith Couchman

MY MOTHER HUDDLED IN BED DYING; SHE COULDN'T SPEAK OR move. But needing to grasp every last moment with Mom, I tried several approaches to comfort and encourage both of us.

Before my mother quit speaking, she uttered the request, "Hold me." So I touched her constantly. I squeezed her hand, stroked her limbs, and climbed into bed and wrapped my arms around her sweltering body. Sometimes we dozed in the hospital bed together. Other times, I slept on the floor while reaching up and holding her hand.

When I needed a break, I told Mom I'd sit quietly in the room. Occasionally, I reassured her of my presence, and sometimes she'd respond with a small stir. But usually I just trusted that she heard me. At times, I quietly played sacred music.

I also talked aloud and whispered into Mom's ear. I recalled good memories, thanked her for loving and raising me, and described how her life had been worthy and worthwhile. I sang her favorite gospel songs. I reminded her how she'd walk with Jesus soon, whole and healthy.

Later, when I consulted a hospice worker, he told me, "You did all the right things. This is what we teach family and friends to do. This is what people in their last stages of life need." I felt I'd fumbled around. But I learned that even if we feel uncertain, awkward, or silly, it's simply our presence that makes the difference.

You can offer dying people the physical presence of someone traveling this last journey with them. A tender touch, other than medical professionals, to comfort them. A quiet atmosphere with visitors focusing on the dying person, not chatting with one another. And the voice of someone who values, thanks, and reassures them.

SWEET TEA FOR TWO

Kathe Wunnenberg

AFTER I MARRIED AND MOVED SEVERAL STATES AWAY FROM FAMILY, I received a call telling me that Grandma's health had worsened. So I prayed, and then I called her.

"Grandma, I'd like to fly back to see you. Should I come now and have sweet tea with you or wait until your funeral?" (My directness may seem harsh, but Grandma and I could talk straight.)

"Come have tea," she chuckled.

So I did.

When I arrived and saw Grandma, her once tall, robust body had withered, and she was now a frail, thin woman with a cane. Over the following few days we rocked on her front porch and sipped sweet tea. We recalled favorite memories and recipes. We talked about heaven and her greeting committee.

A few weeks later, Grandma died. I didn't attend her funeral. Instead, I sipped a long distance glass of sweet tea and thanked God for Grandma. Though some people probably didn't understand, I felt peace in knowing I had given Grandma the gift of my presence.

Living apart from family, especially when aging or health issues arise, can be challenging. When you or someone you know faces this challenge, pray. Ask God to give discernment to know when to go. If appropriate, talk to the ailing relative or other family members about the timing. If traveling there is not possible, ask God to reveal creative ways to help you bring hope to your relative, even from a distance.

PEACH PIE PICNIC

Anne Denmark

MR. KLINE, A CRUSTY, RETIRED JOCKEY, LIVED ALONE JUST DOWN our street. He was my husband Don's patient, and it began the relationship between the Doc and the Jock. It also began his love for my peach pie.

Don would frequently invite him for holiday dinners. And boy, did he ever love my homemade pie! His favorite was peach topped with a sugary lattice and served with clouds of freshly whipped cream.

He would sit and just watch our young boys devour their portions. He had never married and took great delight in our children. Chuckling, he would say, "Sure does eat good, doesn't it, son?" I couldn't tell which he enjoyed most—watching the boys eat theirs or savoring his own flaky bite.

One day, Don called from the hospital with a request. Bake a peach pie to bring to the hospital. Mr. Kline had been admitted and Don knew our friend's pie days were ending.

It was not easy to set aside my seemingly urgent plans, but I did. Next day, I visited with a warm peach pie in a basket for a bedside picnic. His ninety-year-old sister joined us. Between each bite our dying friend pointed up to heaven.

Through the connection of family dinners and pies, Don had asked Mr. Kline if he'd made his peace with God. They prayed and he received the hope of eternal life.

"No eye has seen, what no ear has heard, and what no human mind has conceived—the things God has prepared for those who love him" (1 Corinthians 2:9). I wonder if our friend is eating heavenly peach pie right now.

Support for the dying, of course, includes your presence, prayers, and maybe even a peach pie. But it also can include a gently worded question: Are you ready to see God? What greater joy or responsibility can there be than to help a friend over the doorstep into eternity with Jesus.

WATER FOR THE WILDERNESS

Sofia Roitman Trillo

A FEW YEARS AGO, ANNA WAS HAPPILY ENGAGED. HER DREAM AS A little girl was to be swept away by a handsome man, go on to travel the world, and then settle somewhere in the Midwest with her husband to raise their children. Suddenly, just as a tornado hits without warning, her fiancé broke their engagement. The man she was madly in love with left her without explanation and turned into a stranger.

After four years of pouring her life into him, Anna was devastated. With wedding plans half done and a wedding dress in the closet, the loss of her dreams was too much. She hurled down into a deep despair.

As one of her closest friends, I wasn't sure what to do. My dear friend, who could laugh at herself and make everyone laugh with her, couldn't find joy in everyday life. She was eating very little and having a hard time getting out of bed. What could I do to help her?

As I prayed, a picture came to mind of a wild desert land with clouds forming in the far distance. It would be so difficult to walk through that wilderness, I thought. Then I understood what Anna saw as her life. So what can bring life to the desert? Water, of course!

Each day, I would look for a verse that spoke about hope or of the goodness of God. I would simply text or email it to her with no other words. I also found pictures of luscious vegetation and nature scenes reflecting the beauty God created. Later, she confided to me that the verses or pictures I sent became an anchor of hope.

Do you know someone who needs hope? Let them know you are praying for them, and send them verses like these to bring life to their desert and water to ther soul:

- Psalm 25:5–6; 27:4–5; 33:21–22
- Isaiah 40:31
- Jeremiah 29:11.

PAIN KILLER

Barbara Hunsaker

As a principal of a small Christian school, one phenomenon I saw from time to time was "cutting." Students would cut themselves, not deeply enough to do permanent damage but enough to inflict pain and leave scars. I wondered why students would "cut," and no amount of discussion would help me understand.

Until I experienced depression.

A few years ago, life threw me some pretty tough blows and I began to wonder if I would ever recover. I was in so much pain physically, mentally, and emotionally that I was desperate to make the pain go away. That's when it hit me: "cutting" was a different kind of pain. It could make the pain I was experiencing go away.

I didn't cut myself or do anything else destructive, but God used that experience to help me realize what it was like to hurt—really hurt. I decided right then and there I needed a new perspective.

Psalm 34:18 says, "The LORD is close to the brokenhearted and saves those who are crushed in spirit." Are you feeling brokenhearted? Crushed? Like you can't even breathe? Try this:

- *Pray:* "Lord, I'm so tired of hurting. At times, I feel like I can't take another breath. Please bear this pain with me and let me know I'm not alone."
- *Start a journal:* Tell God how much you are hurting. Include a list of the good things in your life.
- *Make a plan to add something new to your life:* Exercise, a new hobby, attend a Bible study.

Sometimes you may need to seek professional help. Visit your doctor to see whether medication or counseling might be needed to help you climb out of the pit of depression.

Know that God cares for you and that He will help you through this.

⮂ DIABETES ⮀

FROM BEAST TO BLESSING

Robyn Bellerson

WHEN DOCTORS CONFIRMED THE DIAGNOSIS, WE KNEW IT WOULD mean great change for our family. Type I diabetes is not a death sentence, but to an emaciated little girl, afraid of needles and longing to be a basketball star, it may have felt like one. Diabetes was our beast, but it became our blessing.

After days of hospitals and Diabetes 101, I finally sat in my room, alone for the first time since the doctor's visit, and I felt an inexplicable sense of peace come over me. It was the kind of peace that only comes from God and his Word. This diagnosis was not a beast; it was a blessing. Our daughter was going to live. She needed no surgery and no harsh treatments, and she could love and play as she always had. It was beautiful.

In Jeremiah 29:11, the Bible says that God wants to prosper us, not harm us. These words turned our beast into a blessing. Kaitlyn has claimed diabetes as her ministry as she feels that the faith and joy she exhibits in her daily life, even while pricking her finger ten times a day or giving herself a shot before every meal, is putting into practice her faith and trust in God. My husband and I have noted the same thing. People notice our faith. When we are asked about our decision to allow Kaitlyn to continue in competitive sports, people notice. When Kaitlyn travels with her team, people notice. When asked how we do it, our answer is the same as hers. We claim God's promise to tame our beast and make life beautiful.

If you or someone you are close to lives with diabetes, use the regimen of pricking the finger as a "prayer prick," reminding you to "check your spiritual blood sugar" and refuel with the power of the Holy Spirit.

LEADER LIFTER

Kathe Wunnenberg

DURING AN EXTREME TIME OF TRANSITION IN OUR CHURCH, I KNEW our pastors and leaders were discouraged. I prayed and felt the Holy Spirit prompt me to mobilize support. My pastor agreed. The following Sunday during worship, I invited our pastors and leaders to stand at the front of the room. Each one held a bull's-eye target.

"The enemy has a battle strategy," I said. "The church is the target, but the pastors and leaders are the bull's-eye." I explained our need to develop strategic prayer and encouragement for our pastors and leaders. As each person left that day, they received a bull's-eye flier with a picture of our pastor's face on it. On the back were "targeted Scriptures" to pray and a list of ideas to encourage our leaders. A few of the ideas were favorite restaurants, entertainment ideas, bookstores, sporting events, and services needed like lawn care and housecleaning. Over the weeks that followed, many prayers and acts of encouragement were offered to support our leaders.

Pray and ask God to show you at least one leader who is discouraged and target your leaders in your prayers. Encourage him or her with a gift, act of service, or word of affirmation.

As the leader of Hopelifters, I envision myself wearing a bull's-eye too, so I'm intentional about mobilizing prayer and support for myself (see chapter 10). I also look for settings to connect with other Christian leaders. One group I've found is GirlFriendIt, a leadership movement for women. Cofounders Lisa Jernigan and Patty Wyatt spread hope to Christian women in leadership by providing opportunities for them to connect (www.girlfriendit.org).

Amazingly, when leaders are prayed up and encouraged, they continue to spread hope. Look for ways you can lift *your* leaders. And if you're a leader, look for hopelifters to support *you*!

A VERY IMPORTANT DATE

Lisa DeLight

IT'S SAID THE ONLY DIFFERENCE BETWEEN DEATH AND DIVORCE IS that death is final and the last good-bye is indeed the last until you meet again in the heavenly realms. With divorce, there is good-bye, closure, relief, and then, "I will see you next week when I pick up the kids."

Divorce is a mini-death that occurs over and over again. Wounds are reopened until enough time passes that they are completely healed. Don't downplay the hurt of a divorced friend or family member or assume they've had plenty of time to get over it. Instead, come alongside them and pray for them.

Consider asking the person who is grieving through divorce about their significant dates. When is their anniversary? Do they have other significant dates, such as the first date, first kiss, or engagement, which they regularly observed? Make a plan to get through those dates together—and not necessarily with a box of Kleenex.

The greatest kindness I was shown in my divorce was when I told my best friend that my wedding anniversary was approaching and I could not bear the idea of one more occasion to sit around feeling sorry for myself. We planned a date for that day: dinner and a movie. I looked forward to the day for two weeks as opposed to dreading it with every fiber of my hurting self.

Are you close to someone who is dealing with divorce? Ask her if you can help "fill in" those dates with your caring presence and an enjoyable activity.

HEART ATTACK

Janet Drez

I SAT IN THE COURTROOM WITH MY FRIEND FOR THE THIRD TIME. IT appeared her heart-wrenching divorce would at last be final. Watching her hunched shoulders quaking with one more bout of tears, I cried out to God, "Lord, I know you love Liz more than I do, but she's so broken she can't even fathom being loved by you, or anyone else for that matter. What can I do to show her Your love?"

Immediately I envisioned dozens of cut-out hearts. I'm a scrapbooker and knew I had plenty of scraps at home and, of course, a heart-shaped die cut. Once I left Liz in the company of a friend, I raced home and began to cut out hearts. Big ones. Small ones. I pulled out my Bible and began writing down all the passages where God tells us of His love.

"Since you are precious and honored in My sight, and because I love you" (Isaiah 43:4).

"Let Him lead me to the banquet hall, and let His banner over me be love" (Song of Songs 2:4).

On some I simply wrote "I love you" or "You matter to God" or "You are greatly loved." I snuck into Liz's apartment armed with nothing more than my pile of hearts and some tape. I began to tape the hearts everywhere: the bathroom mirror, the kitchen sink, inside the pantry, on the ceiling. It definitely made me smile.

When she returned home the next day, those hearts nearly gave her a heart attack! She left them up for several months, and she told me that they helped her sense God's love in a tangible way. Sometimes the simplest of ideas make for the best hopelifter, especially when your "heart" is in it!

FEEDING ON TRUTH

Gia Chapman

AFTER HEARING A NEWS STORY ABOUT EATING DISORDERS, I REMEM-
ber thinking, *If I'm bulimic, I can never have a baby.*

I was in my twenties. My private battle with food had been wag-
ing since my teenage years. Although I grew up in a godly home
with parents who loved me, I was driven by perfectionism and the
need to control my image. I quickly learned I could control my body
image with food. I starved myself. Later, I resorted to forcing myself
to throw up. My strive for perfection fueled my desire to improve
the way others saw me. This destructive pattern continued until I
decided I needed help to become healthy so I could have a baby.
Finally, through a series of circumstances including dealing with a
past abortion, I hired a personal trainer, who helped me learn the
truth about food. I discovered I could eat the right things, the right
way, and I could be healthy.

I also started feeding myself more of God's truth. Instead of looking into the mirror of human perfection and striving to have the
perfect body image, I was reminded to look through God's eyes to
see myself.

Although I still fight against the perfect body image, now I stop
and ask, "What is the truth?" And I remind myself: "I can do all
things through Him who gives me strength" (Philippians 4:13).

If you know someone struggling with an eating disorder, be
supportive and listen. Educate yourself about eating disorders, and
encourage her to eat healthy foods. Look up verses about body image
and unconditional love. Pray Scripture for her. The battle against
eating disorders can be long and hard, so be patient and understanding; but at the same time, encourage her to seek professional help if
the problem becomes severe.

TRAVEL LIGHT

Kathe Wunnenberg

BEING DISCONNECTED FROM YOUR FAMILY BY DISTANCE OR DIS-agreement, hurts. I understand the pain of both. I've lived several states away for many years and have grieved the loss of togetherness. Yet the pain I've experienced (or caused) from family disunity has been more difficult to endure. Careless words or actions, when not confronted or forgiven, grow into grudges, resentment, and bitterness. The distance between hearts may last for years.

How do I cope with family feuds and stay close in heart?

I carry a backpack when I go to visit.

I got this idea from my friend Lisa Jernigan several years ago at a retreat. She talked about burdens we carry like rocks in a backpack. She emptied her backpack of rocks, each one labeled with a person or situation. She encouraged us to identify the hurts we were carrying and to lay them down at Jesus' feet.

My backpack reminds me to travel light. It prompts me to identify any hurts I may have picked up and need to release. Life is too short to carry hurts and damaged relationships.

For many years, I tried too hard to fix people or situations, and my peacemaking weighed me down and became a heavy burden. I spoke up or stepped in instead of laying down my need to control and allowing God to work in the lives of others in His way and timing. My backpack reminds me to "cast all my anxiety on Him because He cares for me" (1 Peter 5:7) and to pray Jesus' words often, "Father, forgive them, for they do not know what they are doing" (Luke 23:34).

If you know someone who is struggling with family hurts, help them to "travel light." Fill a backpack or tote bag with rocks or small pieces of paper and a black marker. Include an instruction card where you invite them to write down their hurts, then remind them of 1 Peter 5:7 and Luke 23:34.

SPORTS DAD

Kathe Wunnenberg

MY HUSBAND, RICH, LOST HIS DAD UNEXPECTEDLY WHEN HE WAS eight. When father and son functions happened through the years, men from church and his friends' dads always included him. Perhaps that's why my husband has such a heart for Little League baseball and is known throughout our community as a caring coach.

When our next door neighbor and her husband divorced, Rich stepped in and invited her son to be a part of our son's team. He understood what it felt like to be a fatherless child. He drove him to practices and games, and provided snacks and equipment as needed.

One day, Rich got the shocking news that his assistant coach had died suddenly. Rich's first thought was about Chris's eight-year-old son. "I wonder how Jacob is," he said. Then he called Jacob's mom.

Ironically, she told him the first person Jacob asked her to call about his dad's death was "Coach Rich."

Sometimes we go through what we go through, to help others go through what we went through. My husband, Rich, a fatherless child, reached out to spread hope to boys like him.

Get in the game of encouraging fatherless boys or girls. Become a big brother or big sister at a local organization. Invite a fatherless child to play sports or attend an activity with your children. Play catch or shoot baskets. One man I know escorts an extra girl to the annual Daddy/Daughter Dance at school because her dad lives in another state. The possibilities are endless!

SECRET GIVING

Kathe Wunnenberg

"WE LOST OUR BUSINESS, HOME, AND CARS WHEN THE ECONOMY declined," said my new neighbor. She and her husband and four children were renting a home down the street while they rebuilt their life. I'd noticed her husband walked to the nearby grocery store, but didn't realize he had no transportation. Suddenly, I realized why they had weekly garage sales.

Then she started to cry. "It's been so hard," she said.

I hugged her as we stood in my driveway. "Can I pray for you?" I asked.

"Yes," she sniffled.

Later that afternoon, my sons Josh and Jordan were having a Nerf gun war with the boys in the neighborhood. I noticed our new neighbor boys had joined the group and were running and squealing too.

During dinner that night with the family, I shared about our new neighbors.

"What can we do to encourage them and give them hope?" I asked.

"Buy the boys Nerf guns for Christmas!" exclaimed Josh and Jordan. Apparently, our new neighbor boys had to borrow guns for the neighborhood Nerf wars.

Christmas was just a few days away. We agreed to practice the principle in Matthew 6:3, "But when you give to the needy, do not let your left hand know what your right hand is doing," and surprise the family with gifts. My boys shopped for the gifts, wrapped them, and early Christmas morning they delivered them on their doorstep, rang the doorbell, and ran. Breathless, they burst into our home, beaming, knowing they had spread hope to a hurting family.

A few days later there was another Nerf war. This time everyone had a gun.

When someone we know is having financial difficulties, we may be called to help in big ways or small. Don't overlook the way small gestures of targeted giving can bring hope to a hurting heart.

THE ICING ON THE CAKE

Anne Denmark

PATTY CALLED TO ASK FOR MONEY. BETWEEN FRANTIC SOBS, SHE explained it was her young son's birthday. She wanted to take her immediate family out to dinner in our small town to celebrate.

My heart raced for the right words to respond.

Patty was a single mom with two small boys who visited our church, invited Jesus into her life, and entered into the abundant life Christ offered. The request sounded simple, but it wasn't. I had already driven her to the grocery store and paid for numerous bags of food.

My heart did not receive the green light to give financially. Instead my answer was, "No, I can't give you money for a family dinner. What I can do is show you how to have a birthday party for your little boy at home."

I also offered to bake the cake and provide the ice cream. With cleaning supplies, a cake mix, and a package of wrapping paper in hand, I spent the morning cleaning a disarrayed apartment, rearranging furniture, and cutting out Dalmatians from the wrapping paper with the boys. They were delighted to help. Patty watched eagerly as I put the party together.

Her family loved the party and asked what kind of church would help her this way. The icing on the cake for me was her beaming smile several months later when she told me she gave her older son a birthday party all by herself.

Sometimes we offer hope by simply showing someone how to do things for themselves.

PAID IN FULL

Rachel Lewis

MY MOTHER AND FATHER DIVORCED WHEN I WAS TWO. EVER SINCE then, I've been trying to comfort the part of my heart that aches for my daddy. I never lost hope that each year would be the year he'd remember to call on my birthday or Christmas. Every few years I might get to see him, but those visits usually ended in tears.

Forgiving him and being able to get through all the years of disappointment was only possible because of my Savior, Healer, and heavenly Father. Calling on God as my Father wasn't easy. It was hard for me to believe He would never leave me when I didn't have a very good example of that in my life. God used other men as father figures to show me His love for me, and I was able to forgive my earthly father long before he ever apologized.

If someone has hurt you deeply and you need healing, get out a piece of paper. Write down everything you hold against that person and all the things you feel they owe you. These could be tangible things, like something they lost or broke, or something they could never repay, like time from your childhood. At the bottom of the page, write: "Because of what Christ did on the cross, I forgive you and release you from your debt." Sign your name.

Anytime you begin to feel angry with that person, remember that list and that you forgave that person and released them from their debt.

Keep in mind you did not do this for the person who hurt you. You did it for you.

FORGIVENESS IN ACTION

LeAnne Gregory

WHEN I WAS BETRAYED BY A TRUSTED FRIEND, I WAS DEEPLY HURT. Looking for comfort, I picked up my Bible and read these words: "Be kind and compassionate to one another, forgiving each other, just as in Christ God forgave you" (Ephesians 4:32). I tried to muster up the compassion to forgive her, but the ability just wouldn't come. I prayed, "Lord Jesus, help me to forgive!" Immediately, the Holy Spirit reminded me of my own ugly sin and how Jesus had been hurt by it and had forgiven me. He acted on that forgiveness to the point of dying for me. Who was I? Was I better than the sinless Son of God?

Upon choosing to forgive, that decision was tested. My friend became ill, and the church called on me to care for her. I consented, not because I wanted to, but out of obedience to God.

After I had arrived at her house and began cooking and cleaning for her, something beautiful happened! My heart was suddenly filled with love and compassion. It was a miracle! I knew I could not muster up that love; it was the love of Jesus flowing through me. By choosing to obey, I had opened up the faucet of Christ's living water, and it flowed over both of us.

If you have been hurt by a friend or family member, pray, pour out your hurts to God, and ask for the ability to forgive. Read your Bible, listen, and let God speak to you. Humble yourself and be obedient to His direction. What is He telling you to do? Finally, if He asks, perform acts of kindness to demonstrate forgiveness.

GRAND LOVE

Kathe Wunnenberg

"MY DAUGHTER IS IN PRISON."

"My son and daughter-in-law are on drugs."

"My divorced daughter is trying to find work."

"My daughter died."

Each of these situations represent grandparents I know who've stepped in to take care of their grandchildren for a reason, season, or lifetime. Forced into an unexpected role, they willingly opened their hearts and homes instead of opting for foster care. Grandparents like these may be hurting and in need of hope.

"What is your greatest challenge?" I asked one grandmother.

"Time and energy!" she replied. "Keeping up with activities, homework, and technology is hard."

Another grandmother went back to work to cover the additional expenses her income couldn't afford.

Grandparents raising grandchildren are also entrusted with their spiritual care. Timothy's grandmother in the Bible played a significant role in his faith journey. "I am reminded of your sincere faith, which first lived in your grandmother Lois and in your mother Eunice and, I am persuaded, now lives in you also" (2 Timothy 1:5).

How can I spread hope and show "grand love?" I prayed.

Here are a few ideas I've tried:

- Adopt a grandparent for a day, weekend, or holiday.
- Offer your gift of time or services to help. Drive. Cook. Host a play date.
- Host a "grand" shower. Help provide for items the grandparent may need: toys, clothing, or favorite stores or entertainment venues for gift cards.

And always, always, pray for the grandparent.

A CUP OF TEA AND A DVD

Kathe Wunnenberg

"I'M FOCUSING ON WHAT I CAN DO, RATHER THAN WHAT I CAN'T do!" my mom announced one day on the phone. "I can pray. I can cook. I can encourage."

My very active mom was being forced to slow down because of health challenges. Mom's positive attitude about her more restricted life inspired me. To support her homebound ministry, I rallied my brothers to join me to purchase a special seventy-fifth birthday gift for her: a teapot, cups, and a variety of teas. Mom's gift of hospitality and the teapot were a perfect fit. She embraced a new way to share her faith and creatively encourage others. She started inviting one or two at a time to join her for a cup of tea and freshly baked goodies.

One day, I phoned and she said, "I'll have to call you back; we're finishing our tea and getting ready to watch you."

Me? I pondered.

Then I realized the DVD I recently sent her as a Mother's Day gift from a speaking event was now being viewed by a larger audience. Amazingly, God enlarged my intention to hand out hope to my mom and used my mom to spread hope to others.

If you know someone who is homebound, find out what they enjoy. (Do they craft, sew, write, sing?) Find others who enjoy what they do and encourage them to visit. Help them hostess a gathering in their home. Purchase or borrow a movie, Bible study, or a DVD of a favorite speaker. Give them a basket of teas, coffee, and other goodies to serve as refreshments. If they can't go out, help them to gather others in!

HELPING THE HOMELESS NAVIGATE A "DO OVER"

Donna Morris

SEVERAL YEARS AGO I HAD THE PRIVILEGE OF VOLUNTEERING AT MY church with a group of eight individuals. For over a year, we met on a weekly basis with a single homeless mom in an attempt to facilitate real change in her life. We discussed all facets of her life: housing, job goals, budgeting, and health care services, among others. Each volunteer picked an area of expertise that they had a passion for, and we worked together as a group guiding her to develop and meet her goals. We provided practical assistance at every turn.

We also got to know her and her children on a personal basis. We celebrated birthdays and holidays together. We did our best to surround her with love, support, prayers, and a sense of caring that she did not have at that particular time in her life. Knowing her "story" was important, but only to the extent that we understood her beginning. We also understood that her "story" did not have to define her, and she could create a new legacy to pass on to her children that was filled with promise and hope. All of us worked toward that goal.

Sometimes hopelifting is a long-term, complicated process that requires more than one person. When that is the case, as it was here, form a team of people who can offer help together. Give the homeless not just a house, but a "home" by virtue of your caring, coaching, and compassion.

STANDING STONES

Erica Wiggenhorn

My FRIEND HAS AN ALCOVE IN HER UPSTAIRS HALLWAY WHERE SHE displays her "standing stones," memorabilia she has collected to remind her of God's work in her family's life. She has a napkin from her wedding day, a pen with the name of her husband's company engraved on it, her prayer warrior grandmother's lace handkerchief, a hospital bracelet to remember God's healing from cancer, and a funeral program to remember His ultimate healing of her mother when she went home to be with Him. Standing stones. Reminders of when the fingerprints of God were so visible she felt as if He was literally holding her hand tightly in a storm. In the middle of the alcove is a large white stone.

When her children have rotten days at school or ask tough questions, she takes them to that alcove. She reminds them of all of the blessings that God has brought to their family. She walks them through the legacy of faith from which they have come. And she fills them with hope in the promises that they will have their own standing stones, because God is faithful.

The alcove is getting pretty full these days. Her children have started their own "standing stones" collections: napkins from a best friend's birthday party, a soccer medal, a hard-earned A on a math test, and pebbles from a father-son campout.

These things remind us of who God has been to us in our past. His Word gives us a great reminder of who He will be in our future. If you would like to create your own display of God's faithfulness to you and your family, read the story of the stones in Joshua 4. Then choose a corner, table, or a basket to place personal memorabilia that reminds you of God's work in your life.

WHEN A HOPELIFTER NEEDS HOPE

Anne Denmark

THE CAR ACCIDENT LEFT ME HELPLESS. A BROKEN BACK, FRACTURED ribs, lungs filling with blood, and now Bell's palsy. Unable to move, I lay on the hospital bed literally trapped and claustrophobic in my own body. Relentless pain was fast depleting my emotional reserves.

I was alone in my room when the specialist came to tell me the news. Gently he said, "I am concerned about this fragile facial nerve. Your allergy to the drug that prevents swelling is unfortunate. If the swelling continues and the nerve is further damaged, then your slurring, drooling, and inability to close one eye will be permanent." Scared and reeling, I held back tears until he left.

I was hopeless. Me ... always the strong compassionate giver ... had come to the end.

Then suddenly she appeared in the doorway. Arriving at the very moment I needed her most, she was hope in the flesh. Unbelievable! Who told her I was here?

I knew her only as the intercessory prayer warrior of my dearest friend, but I hadn't remembered that this friend of my friend lived close to this hospital so far from my home.

She cupped my wet face in her warm hands and took me to Jesus. Her words echoed Scripture and spoke of His promises. Like a lost lamb, I soaked in His love. On my bedside tray, she left a small devotional, *My Utmost for His Highest*, which became a lifeline of encouragement and healing.

How do I thank my friend for sending her prayer angel to rescue me from despair?

Sometimes it is not possible to actually be with someone, but we can send hope through our powerful network of friends. Friends increase your reach. If you don't know anyone in their area, you might want to contact your church, denomination, or other ministry to find someone who can bring hope to a faraway friend who is suffering.

PRESCRIPTION FOR PAMPERING

Shayla Van Hofwegen

INFERTILITY IS A LESS-THAN-GLAMOROUS ROAD TO TRAVEL. You spend your days, weeks, and even years in and out of doctor's offices, doing things you'd never feel comfortable mentioning to anyone. The doctors prescribe tests and rounds of shots and hormones, all of which make you feel downright unattractive.

I can remember looking in the mirror one day and not recognizing the girl staring back at me. I had lost all desire to get ready in the morning. I didn't care what the doctors and nurses at my appointments thought about my sweatpants and dirty hair.

After I received yet another negative pregnancy test, a close friend of mine offered to take me out for some pampering. She scheduled us manicures and pedicures at a local nail salon. We were able to relax, read tabloid magazines, and chat about what was going on in the lives of celebrities. It was nice to escape my struggles for a few hours.

The best part was I went home feeling beautiful again. The simple act of getting my nails painted started to transform how I was feeling on the inside. My friend knew some time with her at the spa was the perfect prescription for me, and I am forever grateful she took the time to notice that it was exactly what I needed.

Do you have a friend that needs a prescription for pampering? Offer to take her for a manicure or pedicure, or get facials or massages at a spa. Or just have some fun shopping for a new outfit at the mall. Help her rediscover her inner beauty by rediscovering her outer beauty.

ENVELOPE OF ENCOURAGEMENT

Shayla Van Hofwegen

THE PAIN OF NOT BEING ABLE TO GET PREGNANT IS UNLIKE ANY other, and reminders you can't conceive are at every turn. Seemingly every day another friend announces she is pregnant. I would plead with God to allow me the opportunity to be a mom.

One evening I walked to the mailbox. I knelt down to open it, expecting advertisements and bills. Instead, to my surprise, I saw a bright orange envelope.

I smirked as I wondered, *Is it a birthday card or an invitation?* I ripped open the envelope before I made it home. It was a card from my mother—not just any card, but a funny one that talks when you open it. I giggled as I walked home, listening to the little characters tell me how much someone was thinking of me.

With all of the technology and social media available, we rarely take time to sit down and write a note or send a card. It's one of the simplest ways to encourage someone. My mom's card still hangs in my kitchen. It reminds me of how much she loves me and thinks of me. It also encourages me to mail cards to others.

Infertility has a way of stealing joy from your life, so it's beyond helpful when others take time to support you through it. Send some-one longing for a child a heartfelt or humorous card or note to show you care. Affirm God is with them. Offer your prayers. And always avoid comments like:

"Kids are a lot of work; count your blessings you don't have any."

"If you can't get pregnant, enjoy being an aunt."

"Don't worry, you are young. It will happen some day."

Do not minimize anyone's desire for children. Instead, maximize your encouraging support.

ST-ST-ST-UTTERING

Adrienne Schiele

I HAVE STUTTERED FOR AS LONG AS I CAN REMEMBER. IT MADE ME an outcast in school all the way from kindergarten to high school graduation. It's also affected my social life as an adult, as many men do not want to be with a woman who stutters.

Various therapies, techniques, and devices have reduced but not eliminated my stutter. I have also been to charismatic healing ceremonies and have had prayers said and hands laid on me. I have pleaded with God more than three times to take stuttering away from me. As He said to Paul, so He says to me: "My grace is sufficient for you, for My power is made perfect in weakness" (2 Corinthians 12:9).

I have accepted that while I may be able to control it, stuttering will always be a part of who I am. I've also learned that my grandfather, whom I dearly loved and who died when I was very young, was also a stutterer.

God made me this way so I would learn to be reliant on Him and not on myself. I'm told I'm in good company. I've heard that Moses and Winston Churchill were also stutterers. God obviously used them, so He can surely use me. I may not get my name in a history book, but God will be glorified through what He does through me.

When God gives you an affliction, do not be resentful. Instead, have a recipe for success. Ask Him to take it away; but if He doesn't, ask Him how He wants to use it in your life for His glory. Remember, an affliction or disability does not make you defective; only your attitude toward it can make you defective.

MAKING MEMORIES

Kathe Wunnenberg

LIVING APART FROM FAMILY CAN HURT. FINDING WAYS TO STAY CON-
nected can ease the pain. I grew up in a small town and enjoyed life
with cousins, family gatherings, and holidays going to grandparents.
When I married, I moved several states away and could only visit
once or twice a year. I grieved Mom's cooking and simple activities
I'd taken for granted, like birthday parties, barbeques, or watching
kids' sporting events. I've grieved for myself and my kids not having
family in the stands cheering them on.

Perhaps that's why I'm intentional about making memories when
we do see family, especially for the kids.

One year we rented a huge cabin with both of my brothers and
families for an old fashioned Thanksgiving. I bought a board game
and played it with my oldest nephew, Dusty. Now he's a dad, and
I've tried to keep the tradition of giving games or toys going with
his sons, Aidan and Braydan.

For many years, I made swimming at the river and catching
crawdads a tradition with my niece and nephew, David and Brooke.

For several years, I hosted a "cousins slumber party" with Ben,
Amber, and Lauren and my two younger sons. A hotel room with
six of us crammed in two beds, plenty of snacks, and a pool helped
us stay connected and make memories.

When Susie and David flew to Arizona as teenagers, we drove to
California, and made memories.

If you are missing long-distance family, have fun brainstorming
how you can get together this year. Will you travel to see them, have
them come to see you, or meet halfway? What new activity can you
try, or what traditional activity can you continue, but with a twist?
Use your time apart to dream and build anticipation so that your
time together will be fun and memorable.

JUST A TOUCH

Anne Denmark

NEWS OF THE ACCIDENT SPREAD QUICKLY IN OUR SMALL TOWN. A young mother left her three small children buckled in the running van while she took a moment, just a moment, to find what she had forgotten in the house.

The oldest child unbuckled the toddler and opened the door. The toddler fell to the ground as the van rolled backward on the elevated driveway, killing the child instantly. Heartbreaking!

Several months later my husband, Don, a physician, called me. The mom was hospitalized in a hysterical state and nothing would calm her down. He asked me to come.

What could I do? I was new in town. I was not a grief counselor and hadn't met this woman. Help, Lord!

Instinctively, I grabbed a tube of hand lotion on the way out the door. Why? I prayed my way to the hospital. I followed her wails down the hall to her room. She wildly tried to apologize and confess her guilt again. Putting a finger to my lips, I indicated that words were not necessary. Then slowly and gently I smoothed the lotion into her hands. I said nothing. I prayed silently and soon she fell asleep.

The lady in the next bed spoke quietly: "That touch really helped her." I agreed and then asked, "Why are you here?" She responded, "I'm a diabetic and they have to amputate my leg." I had no words. "Would you like some hand lotion?" She did.

Touch powerfully offers hope in times of great loss. Without words it says: "I am here. I care." Thank you, Lord, for your touch.

JUST SHOW UP

Kim Erickson

WHEN OUR THREE-YEAR-OLD SON DIED SUDDENLY FROM COMPLICA-tions with strep throat, family and friends surrounded us. I recall those first weeks with deep gratitude and consider each person a blessing in my life. But I also recall feeling so overwhelmed by all of them. It seemed as if every few minutes someone was asking me a question. "What can I do?" "Can I bring food?" "Do you want me to ...?"

I had no idea what to say. It was all I could do to get dressed and brush my teeth! There were so many decisions to make about funeral arrangements that I could not face one more decision, no matter how small it seemed.

If you know someone who has lost a child, she probably is feeling overwhelmed on top of the mountain of grief. So how can you offer her hope? Just show up. Just be there. It truly does not matter whether you do anything. Just show up at her house and sit next to her. You do not need to say anything; just hold her hand and pass the tissues. If being still or quiet feels uncomfortable to you, then just do whatever comes to mind, but do not ask her about it! Go ahead and cook, clean, shop, do the laundry, organize the cards and flowers, or start the "thank you" cards. She will not remember much from this time, but she will remember that you showed up for her. And showing up is all that matters.

GOD'S COMFORT

Kim Erickson

LIVING THROUGH THE LOSS OF OUR THREE-YEAR-OLD SON IS TEACH-ing me a lot about the comfort of God. It took several years after our son died for me to be able to hear people talk about "God's plan" being perfect or that "all things work together for my good" without a strong reaction. I know that people were trying to ease my pain with Bible verses filled with hope. But I must admit that I sometimes wanted to punch them in the mouth! If you know someone who has lost a child, let me encourage you to withhold sharing verses about God's plan for later. Much later.

Scripture that touched my pain during those early years had more to do with God's comfort, His promises, and His infinite hope. It is too difficult for someone who has lost a child to contemplate any plan, even God's plan, which involves so much pain. Instead, share verses that acknowledge her pain and offer God's comfort. It's the only thing that has a chance at filling the giant hole in her heart.

A friend gave us a beautiful photograph with this verse: "The Lord is close to the brokenhearted and saves those who are crushed in spirit" (Psalm 34:18). I used to see it and cry out, "O God, be close to me; let me feel Your presence so that I don't feel so much of this pain."

When I felt crushed in spirit, I begged God to save me from it. In times of her greatest pain, your friend is likely to cling to a thoughtful keepsake or a simple note with words of God's comfort and hope.

GIFT OF REMEMBRANCE

Kathe Wunnenberg

I WENT TO SEE MY AUNT WILMA AFTER HER DAUGHTER CRYSTAL'S death. She welcomed me with a holiday hug, a smile, and a Dr. Pepper—her family's favorite drink. I followed her into the formal living room, where family photos adorned the wall, and we settled in for our annual "Christmas chat." I handed her a present and she squealed with delight when she discovered it was a snowman afghan.

"Crystal loved snowmen," she said as she swiped a tear. "It's hard to believe they're *all* gone now," she sighed.

She recalled her recent trip to the cemetery to decorate the graves of her two adult daughters and her husband of more than fifty years, Uncle June. As hard as I tried, I couldn't imagine her insurmountable grief and feelings of aloneness. But I offered what I could—an afternoon of remembrance. We shared meaningful and humorous stories. We laughed and shed a few tears. We sipped soda while we listened to Crystal's music and songs. We talked about heaven and how sometimes God's ways are mysterious.

Before I left, I embraced my aunt and prayed for her, part of my farewell routine. Then she looked up with a twinkle in her eye and said, "I just love when you come; it makes me feel like Jesus and Crystal were both here."

When someone you know is grieving the loss of an adult child, pray about giving her the gift of remembrance. Offer your presence and listening ear for a moment, afternoon, or occasion. Listen or exchange stories about her child. Take along her child's favorite snack or drink to share. As the Holy Spirit leads: Laugh. Cry. Eat. Pray. Be ready to point her to Jesus and recall what He's done to defeat death. Remind her He is with her always and she will never be alone.

STICKY NOTE TRUTH

Andra Good

WHEN MY BEST FRIEND OF TWENTY YEARS DIED IN A TRAGIC CAR accident at age thirty-five, I found myself feeling hopeless, grief-stricken, and fearful. Leigh Ann was a light in my life, my right hand, and a truth teller. She laughed at my jokes, we enjoyed the same pastimes, and we lived life together well. She had seen me through abandonment by my father, infertility, surgeries, and many other difficult life experiences. But she also walked with me through refinement, the journey of adopting my two beautiful daughters, and healing from physical pain. She held me to God's truth by living it out in her own life and speaking it into mine.

Without Leigh Ann, who would speak truth to me? Her messages of love, laughter, and genuine sincerity were quickly missed. The thought of living without her influence caused me to weep.

Hearing of my pain, a dear Christian friend came for a quick visit. She asked my permission to go through my Bible and then sat on my couch thumbing through the pages. When she was done working, she placed my Bible in my hands. It was marked with dozens of neon-colored sticky notes. Each note was placed next to passages about grief, peace, or comfort and marked with its reference. She prayed over me and my Bible, asking that God's truth would walk me through this pain.

Leigh Ann died two and a half years ago, and my sticky notes are still in place. They're a reminder that the truth my dear friend Leigh Ann spoke into my life was readily available in God's Word.

STARTING OVER SHOWER

Kathe Wunnenberg

"I'VE LOST EVERYTHING IN A FIRE!" SOBBED CAROL.

I listened as she poured out her story of barely escaping the fire that burned her house to the ground. Carol was a middle-aged, single woman who attended the workplace ministry where I served. We were having a luncheon later that day, so I invited her to come as she was.

When Carol got off the elevator, she was wearing her bathrobe and pink furry slippers. She shuffled into our Christian Business Women luncheon on the twenty-sixth floor that overlooked downtown Phoenix.

I invited Carol to come forward and share her story with the group. She also shared from Isaiah 43:2, a timely verse of hope: "When you pass through the waters, I will be with you; and when you pass through the rivers, they will not sweep over you. When you walk through the fire, you will not be burned; the flames will not set you ablaze."

I prayed for Carol, then I invited the group to help as they could. Amazingly, she received several hundred dollars that day to help with basic needs. Then a few women decided our ministry should host a "Starting Over Shower" for Carol. So we did. We sent out invitations with a specific list of items for women to purchase and an opportunity to contribute to a large group gift of a table and chairs. What an amazing time it was to be on the giving side and watch Carol receive hope for a fresh start.

Regardless of the circumstances, losing a home and/or possessions can be painful. Consider hosting a "Starting Over Shower." Obtain a list of items/services the person needs, then invite others to a party where you can address those needs. Not only will you take care of practical needs, but you will also soothe the deeper emotional wounds of loss by offering your caring words and presence.

FILL HER ARMS

Kathe Wunnenberg

I CALLED THE HOSPITAL GIFT SHOP AND ASKED THE WOMAN TO describe the stuffed animals for sale. I listened carefully, then chose the one I felt my friend would like best. Then I asked her to deliver it along with a card inscribed with this message:

> *Shelly,*
> *I'm praying for you. Here's something to fill your arms when you leave the hospital.*
>
> > *Love,*
> > *Kathe*

I'd only known Shelly for a few weeks. With her friend's urging, she contacted me after learning I'd carried and lost a child with the same fatal birth defect as her unborn baby. Like Mary seeking Elizabeth's companionship while carrying a special child, Shelly sought mine. We connected regularly during her pregnancy. I planned to support her during her labor and delivery, but was out of town. Instead, I sent hope from afar.

I recalled the day after my baby died. I wasn't prepared for the painful experience of leaving the hospital. As I sat in a wheelchair in the main lobby waiting to be wheeled outside, I saw another woman in a wheelchair coming toward me. When the attendant pushed her right beside me, I could see she was smiling and holding a newborn baby. Choking back tears, I looked down and realized my arms were empty.

I vowed I would never let another woman I knew experience the pain of leaving the hospital with empty arms. That's why I sent the bear to Shelly, to fill her arms with *something* to hold.

When someone you know loses an infant, pray for God to fill her grieving heart with His comfort and peace. Then invite Him to show you how to fill her arms with meaningful hope. A stuffed animal or a pillow with an inspirational quote or Scripture on it may be just the comforting touch she needs.

SUPPORT TEAM

Kathe Wunnenberg

"I LOST MY JOB!"

I was jolted by my husband's words.

Later that morning when he arrived home, I hugged him, then listened to him share the details of this unexpected happening. His position was eliminated due to budget cuts in defense spending.

I encouraged him to take time to grieve the loss of his job. Over the next few days emotions surfaced—disbelief, fear, anger, and sadness. Questions flooded our minds. How would we survive? My income could not sustain us. What steps should we take?

When someone you know loses a job, here's how you can offer hope in their unemployment:

Pray and enlist others to pray. "I know the plans I have for _____, declares the Lord ... plans to give hope and a future" (Jeremiah 29:11). Invite God to open the person's heart to be willing to trust, have courage, and persevere.

Grieve the loss. Job loss hurts. Feel the pain.

Replenish. Losing a job is emotionally draining. If you have a cabin or time share, offer it to the person for a weekend or a week away for rest and refocus.

Give personal favorites. Make a meal, yummy dessert, or provide a gift card to a favorite restaurant, sporting event, movie, or bookstore. If the person has a hobby, show up with supplies.

Develop strategic support. Enlist people or organizations like Career Connectors (www.careerconnectors.org) to help. Who offers expertise in résumé writing? Interviewing? Human resources? Job search? Life coaching? Personal finance?

Don't offer advice unless asked. Be sensitive to how and when to offer ideas.

Celebrate the small stuff. Job hunting is hard work. Acknowledge accomplishments. Go for ice cream.

Finally, if you are a colleague as well as a friend of the person who lost their job, be sensitive to their hurt but do not avoid them. Reassure them that your friendship will continue outside the workplace, then take steps to make sure that happens.

THANKSGIVING

Kathe Wunnenberg

WHEN I ANNOUNCED MY RESIGNATION FROM MY MINISTRY POSITION where I served for thirteen years, people were shocked. Many tried to convince me to stay; however, I knew God had called me to go.

My goal was to leave well and to let go gracefully. I sought wisdom from other leaders. My friend Nancy compared losing a ministry to an amputation. Having served as a pastor's wife for many years, Nancy understood the joy of growing a church and the sorrow of releasing one. She told me to prepare for friendships to be cut off when I departed. She also encouraged me to set aside a season of time after I left to celebrate and thank God for what He had done.

So I did.

I declared "Thanksgiving" in January, the month I left. I purchased a new journal to record my harvest of blessings and a stack of thank-you cards. I invited God to bring to remembrance each day people, significant happenings, and lessons I learned through that ministry. As He did, I wrote each "thanksgiving memory" down in my journal. I swiped a tear or two as I recognized God's goodness through the years for what He had done.

Sometimes I felt a need to write a note to personally thank someone for how God used that person in my life. I usually included Philippians 1:3, "I thank my God every time I remember you," in the thank-you card. This journey of gratitude was healing as I grieved the ministry I left.

If you know someone who is leaving or has lost a ministry, encourage them to take time to reflect over the past years, grieve over the losses, and rejoice at the accomplishments. And, consider giving her a package of thank you cards, stamps, and a journal.

MEMORIAL MEAL

Judith Couchman

LIKE MANY FAMILIES SPREAD ACROSS THE COUNTRY, MY MOTHER and I lived in different states. When Mom grew ill, I traveled back and forth to Phoenix, Arizona, wanting to help usher her peaceably toward heaven. Between keeping up with work via a laptop and tending to Mom, I couldn't inform all my friends about her progress and other details.

After Mom's death, my family traveled to Omaha, Nebraska, for a mortuary visitation and then to rural Iowa for the burial. Once again, I couldn't keep my friends informed. Yet, I urgently wanted to process what happened and to talk about my mom.

Somehow, my friend Laurel intuitively sensed this even without talking to me. After I returned home, she hosted a potluck dinner in my mother's honor and invited a half dozen of my closest friends to attend. During the dinner, I relived recent events: the last days and moments with Mom, the immediate aftermath of her death, and the trips to finally bury her beside my father in a family cemetery.

Later, seated on a couch with dessert and coffee, I talked about my mother: everything from favorite hobbies to spiritual beliefs to silly foibles. I shared photos of Mom at different ages and read her handwritten note about wanting to dwell with Jesus. Overall, the "memorial meal" fed me hope. This hope bolstered me to believe Mom would be remembered and I would recover from the deep pain.

Sometimes, the best thing you can offer a grieving person is a listening ear as she remembers her lost loved one and processes her pain.

MORNING'S GLORY

Starr Ayers

"WEEPING MAY STAY FOR THE NIGHT, BUT REJOICING COMES IN THE morning" (Psalm 30:5).

It was the morning after my mother's death, and I was leaving our driveway for the first family viewing. As I choked back my tears, I glanced to one side and brought my car to an abrupt halt. Several "Wine and Roses" bushes are planted in the front corner of our yard. I've never had an affinity for these bushes. They are only pretty in season. The rest of the year they simply look like *dead* bushes. This morning was different. Engulfing these seemingly lifeless bushes was a beautiful host of pink and purple morning glories.

I threw open the car door and rushed into the house for my camera. Kicking off my shoes, I ran barefoot across the morning's freshly sprinkled lawn, snapped the photos, and hurried back inside to get my daughter. I wanted her to witness this unmistakable morning miracle. Accompanying her into the front yard, I told her of my aversion for these dead-looking bushes and of how the morning glories had swallowed them up. As each word left my tongue, they resounded in my head as God whispered in my spirit: *I have swallowed up the death with the morning's glory.*

Overwhelmed by the assurance my mother was in the company of her Lord, I dropped my head. Then, noticing my wet, grass-covered feet, I realized my shoes were off. I was standing on holy ground!

If you are grieving, be alert to the creative and unexpected ways God sends His comfort—through a hug, a card, a verse that touches your heart, a happy memory. God is present in your grief if you only look for Him.

MY MEMORABLE MUTTS

Adrienne Schiele

I HAVE EXPERIENCED THE LOSS OF A PET SEVERAL TIMES OVER THE years: from natural death, accidents, euthanasia, and giving them away. Oddly, the most difficult of the four is the last. I felt like I was giving away a child and had somehow let my dog down. However, we were moving, and the new home would not have a fenced backyard for Mandy. Even though I knew she was going to a good home, it was still one of the hardest things I've ever had to do.

Nolan had to be euthanized. He had cancer, which had been removed once, but recurred with a vengeance. He was suffering.

Van Buren was my childhood pet who died of poisoning when I was six. I was devastated. He'd meet me at the bus stop nearly every day and was my constant companion.

Through all this, I've learned how much God loves animals. He takes the time to design each one as He sees fit. Just look at all the different breeds and sizes of dogs!

The loss of a pet is unique, because unlike the loss of a fellow human, the pet loves us unconditionally no matter what our mood, financial status, or weight. There is always genuine acceptance. Even in the best of human relationships, there are still times of strife and conflict.

So what's the recipe to help someone heal from losing a pet? Validate their pain. Send a card and mention a special memory with the pet. Purchase a pet ornament with the lost pet's name. Frame a picture of the lost pet. Or give a stuffed animal similar to the one lost.

Finally, if appropriate, surprise the person with a new pet. You'll never replace the lost pet, just transfer the love.

NO STRINGS ATTACHED

Brenda Evans

WHEN MY HUSBAND DIED FROM A SUDDEN RECURRENCE OF CANCER, I needed to stop the world so that I could come to terms with the road ahead.

We draw strength from the support of friends and family, but while some widows draw strength from being surrounded by loved ones, I needed the quiet with the Lord to find my inner strength. I knew that my friends and family would understand my need for solitude to walk through my grief.

I was blessed by the ways my friends and family loved me. They did not ask for my time as my energy was drained from my grieving. They had no expectations. No strings attached, just love.

My neighbor sent her children with gifts of food and smiles. She sent warm cocoa in the evening, and one morning, a warm breakfast. Dinner sometimes. No long conversations, just kindness.

A former student and his wife surprised me with a gift left on my doorstep. Imagine my delight when I found a metal work of art I had admired, made by his hands and given with love.

My family made sure I had groceries and, when I was ready, was there to meet for dinner. No questions about the future, just food and conversation and love.

My close childhood friends continued to meet for breakfast once a month when I was ready, bringing normalcy and hope.

Our coworkers sent cards and offers of meals. I received messages by texts, email, mail, or Facebook daily.

The love of Jesus was evident in these gifts. Gifts of love, perfectly planned to fill the needs of a hurting friend—with no strings attached.

CELEBRATING LIFE

Brenda Evans

PLANNING THE MEMORIAL SERVICE OF A SPOUSE IS THE MOST DIF-
ficult thing a widow can do. The details of the service and the reception take careful planning.

The bubble of grace the Lord wrapped around me after the death
of my husband helped me get through those early days of sorrow.
Our church, Christian school, and family helped me with the planning and implementation of our "Celebration of Life." My husband
was a vibrant middle school teacher who left behind a large number
of grieving students and families. My goal was to help my family and
these friends celebrate his joyous life in Christ.

The pastor held a meeting with the principal of the school and
her staff, my family, and the planners at the church to prepare for
our service and reception. In the meeting, I was asked what I envisioned, and every time I would express an idea, they would plan to
make it happen. They continued to express what an honor it was
to be able to help with his service. I was so moved by their spirit of
love and compassion for us! The stress of planning would have been
overwhelming had it not been for these caring friends.

The service and reception were flawless. A coordinator was in
place to care for my family. My sister and the school staff organized
the meal, the memorabilia, the photo montage, and the posters the
students made. Food flowed from the school families. My worries
were nonexistent as love overflowed. The Spirit of the Lord was
evident in the way God's people responded to a widow's need.

While any time of bereavement requires an army of helpers, it
also entails a need for colonels and generals! If you have a talent for
organization, you might help with planning meetings and coordi-
nating volunteers for the memorial service and afterwards. If not,
check whether your bereaved friend has the organizational support
she needs by contacting her church, workplace, or other family
members.

SHE DOES MY DISHES

Alonna Hoogesteger

WHEN MY HUSBAND DIED SUDDENLY IN MY ARMS, I IMMEDIATELY felt numbness and deep pain, knowing I had lost a great part of myself. Thinking was so hard. My brain was in a fog.

During the days that followed, my dear friend Rhonda would come over and, as part of her visit, would do my dishes. This was a burden lifted, a simple task, but monumental to me. She would talk if I talked or was silent if I had no words. It was not her conversation, knowledge, or prayers that initially made the difference, but her peaceful and loving presence. Rhonda helped to fill the emptiness.

God gives everyone different gifts, passions, and talents. Through these qualities she ministered to me. Rhonda is a quilter, and she immediately started the "mourning quilt." That quilt represents our children, couples in our church group, and seasons in our lives. She designed and prayed over every stitch, a treasured gift.

Rhonda loves to send cards—funny ones to Kleenex box cards. On January 22, I received my first card, letting me know she loved and cared about me and my family. Wouldn't you know, I received a card for a year on the twenty-second of each month, marking the day of my husband's death. She remembered.

As time passed, we've talked about that very special time and how it helped both of us in our grieving process. She shared feelings of not knowing what to do or say, but in listening to the Holy Spirit, she responded and comforted me as well as herself.

PASS ON YOUR FAITH

Kathe Wunnenberg

"Mr. Evans has cancer."

When this news spread about the middle-school Bible teacher at Bethany Christian School, our school community was devastated. Everyone loved Mr. Evans. His quick wit, authenticity, prayers, and fearless faith were contagious. His concern for others and influence went far beyond the classroom. He and his wife, Brenda, treated students and staff like family. They invested deeply in individuals and spent most weekends attending student sporting events or performances.

The staff cried out to God. Our school community worked together to provide support while Mr. Evans endured surgeries and treatment. Some did yard work and cleaned house. Others gave financially. Many prayed, sent cards, or wrote online encouragement. One student's mom was the substitute teacher for most of the year. Students rallied together to pray. They believed God would heal Mr. Evans. They declared a "Mr. Evans Day" and wore his favorite color, pink.

Word came that Mr. Evans was near death. Students rallied to send him a farewell video with personal messages. The next day, Mr. Evans was ushered into heaven. The school community grieved his loss. The staff cried out to God again, and this time He delivered creative compassion through a box of leftover t-shirts. The staff surprised the students with commemorative Mr. Evans t-shirts emblazoned with the Lone Ranger, a favorite of Mr. Evans.

At Mr. Evans's "Celebration of Life" multitudes gathered to worship and thank God for his life, including several students wearing his ties. As students exited the service, each one received a turquoise metal baton with Hebrews 12:12: "Let us run with perseverance the race marked out for us. Let us fix our eyes on Jesus." My son Josh treasures this gift. It reminds him of his teacher's faith—a lasting legacy passed on to my son, inspiring him to do the same.

When a school suffers a loss of a teacher, look for creative, compassionate, tangible ways to help the students grieve their loss. In our case, we used t-shirts, ties, and batons. What could you use?

JESUS-WITH-SKIN-ON FRIEND

Anonymous

I'VE BEEN MARRIED MANY YEARS TO THE SAME MAN. FOR MOST OF our marriage, I've hurt. I've endured my husband's anger and disrespect that he directed toward me. After much counsel and prayer I made the decision to move out. I knew God was with me, but I felt alone and afraid.

During this difficult time, a dear friend became the hands and feet of Jesus to me. Here are a few things she did:

- She listened to me and validated my feelings.
- She gave me permission to feel sad, angry, and hurt.
- She didn't judge my feelings.
- She offered her home to me so I would have a safe and quiet place to stay.
- She helped me move.
- She texted or called me a few times daily.
- She told me she was praying for me every day.
- When I had a need, she met it.

When I think about my friend, she was really Jesus to me. She showed love, compassion, and kindness, but she also spoke truth about my life. She helped me through this difficult time.

After a few weeks, much prayer, and meditating on Scripture, I decided to return to my husband and our home. I'm hopeful the Lord will give us His grace to be the couple He wants us to be.

Things needed to help someone with marriage challenges:

- *A listening ear* (to hear her hurts).
- *A phone* (to text, call, or tell her you are praying).
- *Your hands* (to hug her, wipe a tear, or point her to professional help or God's truth).
- *Your feet* (for acts of service she may need).

ASK YOUR FIRST HUSBAND

Kathe Wunnenberg

"IT'S OVER!" THE WOMAN SOBBED.

I listened to her share her painful journey of her husband's rejection. Her intentional efforts to be a godly wife, seek counseling, and even offer to separate temporarily appeared to be hopeless. Her husband was unwilling to try and wanted to end the marriage.

"I know God hates divorce," she sniffled. "What am I supposed to do?"

After a long pause, I replied, "Ask your First Husband."

She looked puzzled.

I shared my story of receiving this advice from a friend, Nancy Ray, a few years earlier when I was struggling in my marriage. For many years, I felt Rich's career, sporting events with kids, and watching television ranked higher than me. I longed for quality time, deep spiritual conversation, and meaningful ministry *together*; yet I felt rejected and unloved, repeatedly.

Then Nancy pointed me to Isaiah 54:5: "For your Maker is your Husband—the LORD Almighty is His name—the Holy One of Israel is your Redeemer; He is called the God of all the earth."

What do I have to lose? I thought. Finally, after nearly three decades of marriage, I realized I couldn't change Rich. I released my expectations and invited my First Husband to help me persevere. Nancy's simple advice gave me hope to trust the One who made me and knew me. Now, instead of expecting Rich to meet all of my needs, I cry out to God, my First Husband. He always listens and responds with His truth. He often surprises me with unexpected love gifts of rain in the desert or wildflowers along a creek bank, something Rich could *never* do.

In the midst of any marriage struggle is God, your First Husband, who loves and never leaves. I've shared this idea with many of my single and divorced friends, too. Here's my standard greeting to them: "So how's your First Husband treating you?"

NEW SONG

Shelly Watkins

A SONG IS A POWERFUL THING. I'M FASCINATED WITH THE ABILITY of a song to draw me to worship in the presence of the Lord.

Perhaps, not surprisingly, I married a singer. He sang with a band on the weekends, and after a whirlwind romance he composed a song and sang at our wedding ten months later. We were young and naïve enough to be happy at first. However, after thirteen years and five children, the winds and rains of life caused the spiritual house we had built on sand to come crashing down. The fall was great, ending in divorce.

While trying to start a new life in a new place, I never felt so alone and abandoned. It was during this time I began attending church and truly seeking the Lord. He began to show me that regardless of the fact that I blamed my husband, I was a sinner in need of salvation. Jesus sang His song of love over me when I felt unloved. He poured out grace and mercy when I felt pitifully broken and worthless. I heard His sweet song in the beautiful hymns of old, in contemporary songs, and in the Word, especially the Psalms.

About six months later, I received a phone call. It was my ex-husband, and he told me the Lord sang the same songs over him. We made arrangements to meet, and he repented and sought forgiveness from the children and me. It was a long road, but we were able to build a new foundation together on Christ and remarried.

When you encounter someone who is experiencing marriage challenges, encourage her to seek healing and hope in God's presence, perhaps through the gift of song or worship. God will reveal the off-key thoughts, actions, or attitudes that may need to be tuned to His truth. She may discover her need to seek repentance or spiritual renewal and her need for the church—people like you and me—to help her heal. A timely Scripture, encouraging word, prayer, or even a Christian song may restore her hope and perhaps even her marriage. Not every marriage struggle will end in divorce and remarriage; however, every heart yielded to God will find healing, hope, and perhaps even a new song.

LOOKING PAST THE STIGMA

Deb Niehof

WHEN OUR DAUGHTER HAD HER FIRST BIPOLAR EPISODE, SHE WAS living in California and we were in the Midwest. It was obvious that she needed our care, so we brought her home and helped her receive the medical attention that she needed. That first year was rough, with two hospitalizations, countless trips to the psychiatrist, and numerous medication changes. We were with her around the clock, partly because we were concerned about her safety, and partly because she was anxious about being left alone. This kind of care giving was wearing, but we did have rays of hope and support along the way.

Our church family is small and close. We decided, with our daughter's permission, to share a bit of what we were experiencing. Although not everyone understood what mental illness was, there was an outpouring of love and care. People brought meals, sent cards, and asked what they could do to help. The deacons put together a list of people who would be willing to spend time with our daughter so that my husband and I could get away. In talking to other families affected by mental illness, I know that this kind of support is not always the case. I think that because we were open about the situation and our needs, our fellow church members looked past the stigma often associated with mental illness and reached out as they would to any family in need.

One of the things that helped me the most was to talk with another woman whose daughter had been diagnosed with bipolar disorder several years earlier. I will always be grateful to the friend who put us in touch with each other, as there is nothing quite like talking to someone who has had the same experience and can completely understand the issues you are facing. I am thankful that I am able to do that for others now in my work with the National Alliance on Mental Illness (NAMI). I am also thankful that with appropriate medication and a healthy lifestyle, our daughter is now doing well.

THE NEED TO BE HEARD

Erinn Kanney

AS A THERAPIST, I OFTEN DEAL WITH MENTALLY ILL CLIENTS IN DIS-
tress. Once a client ran off because she was scared. When I caught
her, I asked, "What's wrong?" She shared what she was hearing in
her head. I told her I was sorry and that hearing such things must be
scary. She looked at me and said, "Yes, it's scary." I encouraged her
to think about her favorite song and share it with me to drown out
the voices. She started singing and calmed down.

That day I learned an important lesson: with anyone who is suffering from a mental illness, acknowledge the feelings and the fears
first. After they feel heard, then you can give counsel.

Another time a client in a psychotic episode was seeing horrible things and screaming. I acknowledged her fears, then asked,
"What can we do if we're afraid?" She replied, "I can pray to Jesus."
I reminded her that whenever she heard voices in her head or saw
people in her mind who overwhelmed her, she could cast them out
in Jesus' name. She agreed and shared her fears with me, and we
lifted them to Jesus. The next day, she said she slept for the first time
in a long while, because Jesus was standing at the foot of her bed
keeping her safe. She was peaceful compared to the day before.

Listening is also key to bringing hope to someone who has a family member with mental illness. We need to support families going
through this trauma, because mental illness is still a stigma, and our
society doesn't provide enough resources. Finding proper help for the
mentally ill—the right therapist, medication, treatment program—
can be an uphill battle. Families need people on their side to offer
prayer and an attentive ear. Be a listening, caring presence both to
those who are ill and to those who love them.

DON'T FORGET US

Becky J. Miller

WHENEVER MILITARY PERSONNEL ARE DEPLOYED, FAMILY MEMBERS are left behind. Not all soldiers are married, but for those who are, this is a difficult time, counting the days until your loved one is coming home. Perhaps they have been in a combat zone overseas or simply deployed on a training mission. Those spouses and children may need your support.

There are several ways to get involved and help the spouse cope with the separation. Offer free baby-sitting services; take them dinner one night; offer to help clean their house. Perhaps mowing the grass would be welcomed, especially for ladies left behind. Going shopping for them can also be rewarding and even fun. Just knowing someone else cares makes a world of difference and brings them hope and helps time pass more quickly.

If you are not near a military installation, you can still give a much needed donation to the American Red Cross designated for the Armed Forces or to the United Service Organizations (USO), which provides centers for military personnel worldwide, primarily in airports. You can adopt a soldier by sending cards and letters, or remember our armed forces in your prayers.

The military is a unique way of life, and I would not trade it for the world. Those who sacrifice their lives and spend months away from their loved ones should be remembered daily in our prayers, and so should their families.

There is a saying: "If you love your freedom, thank a vet." It was my honor to serve my country for six years, and later to serve as a military spouse supporting my husband and sons. If you are in the service, may God bless you!

HOPE IN A GROCERY BAG

Erica Carlson

ON A WARM SPRING MORNING, I ARRIVED AT MY PARENTS' HOUSE, A place I often visited as a twenty-year-old wife with a husband deployed in Iraq. When I arrived at the door, there was a grocery bag, its sides rounded from fullness, sitting outside with my name written on it. With a good deal of curiosity, I carried the bag inside and set it on the table.

With the warm sunshine pouring on me, I explored the contents of the bag. Inside were a few gifts and notes of encouragement. To my lonely heart, it seemed as though some of the gifts were in sets of two, sets of coffee mugs or key chains, which was an encouragement in and of itself, reminding me of my faith that my husband would be coming home and we would be able to share those items together.

The words of encouragement came in a variety of styles and pre-sentations as well. There were poems about the sacrifice and service of having a spouse in the military; others were about the joy of marriage. One poem was rolled up with a little bow tied around it like a scroll, and one piece was on green paper.

I still don't know who sent the mystery bag, but its purpose was served. It provided hope and encouragement to a lonely military wife. The notes of encouragement I still hold dear as I remember that time of inspiration during my "time in the desert." There was nothing too extravagant about the gift or its wrappings; it was the hope in the gift that was meaningful.

MISSION REACH OUT AND RESTORE FAITH

Kathe Wunnenberg

ONE MORNING I WOKE UP THINKING ABOUT A SPECIAL SOLDIER friend who serves in the airborne infantry. Although we'd never met, his words affected me deeply. We connected briefly through email when I requested his approval for a story I'd written. His reply? Permission granted. Then he shared "the rest of the story." His words pierced my heart and opened my eyes to combat horrors and its lingering effects on soldiers. Unexpected tears trickled down my cheek.

"Going to war has made me cold to emotions and even to faith."

His gut-level honesty enlarged my compassion for soldiers fighting outward and inward battles. Calloused hearts and suicide are their growing enemies.

"My challenge to you is: to put faith back in those who lost it from a tragic event."

He said many soldiers need help. They lose a friend or their spouse leaves them. They feel as if no one cares.

"If your prayer group could let them know they're not alone, it would mean a lot to me and to them."

So I accepted his challenge, realizing it's too big for me. Will you join me in this mission to reach out and restore faith to soldiers who secure our freedom? One simple act can make a difference.

"Be patient and don't push your faith. Listen and minimize questions. Pray and let soldiers know you care. Don't quit and stay in touch with your soldier. And, enlist others to help you."

I've also discovered helpful resources you may wish to explore:

www.operationwearehere.com (Christian military themed resources)

www.adoptaussoldier.org (soldiers can sign up for support and others can adopt them)

www.momsinprayer.org (start or join a military moms prayer group)

Finally, use God's Word to reach out. Pray it or send it to a soldier. God's Word is truth and brings hope, healing, freedom, and victory. (Use the verses of hope on pages 237–240 or your own.) Enlist others to pray it with you. Together, with God's help, let's reach out and restore a soldier's faith.

VALIDATE THEIR LOSS

Kathe Wunnenberg

"I NEVER KNEW THIS CHILD FULLY, SO WHY DO I GRIEVE SO DEEPLY? I never held this tiny baby, never saw the sleeping face, never locked eyes and gazed into the soul of this little person. Yet, I feel as if a part of me has died and left a void in my being. Most people don't seem to understand, and they minimize my loss instead of validating my pain from losing this nameless child. Will I always feels so lonely and misunderstood? Is it normal to mourn someone I never knew or lost so long ago? Only when I gave myself permission to grieve the loss of my child did I begin to pick up the pieces of my broken heart and start to heal."

These words from the introduction of my book *Grieving the Child I Never Knew* still comfort me as I think about my three babies lost through miscarriage. Psalm 139:13–16 validates their lives:

> For You created my inmost being;
>> You knit me together in my mother's womb.
> I praise You because I am fearfully and wonderfully made;
>> Your works are wonderful,
>> I know that full well.
> My frame was not hidden from You
>> when I was made in the secret place,
>> when I was woven together in the depths of the earth.
> Your eyes saw my unformed body;
>> all the days ordained for me were written in Your book
>> before one of them came to be.

Validating their lives continues. When my young son suggested we name our unborn babies, we did: Zachary, Matthew, and Luke. On Mother's Day and due dates, I send a card to other women who've lost babies. At Christmas, I help needy children the same age mine would be. All these things help me remember and celebrate their lives.

CALENDAR OF CARE

Erica Wiggenhorn

I STOOD IN THE LIVING ROOM AND STARED AT THE BARE WALLS. My children were born here. My dearest friends in the world lived right around the corner. How in the world was I going to leave this place?

Our church friends had a good-bye party for us. They presented us with a silver photo frame that held three-by-five photos that could be inserted and flipped like a desk calendar. There were thirty pages in all. They collected favorite verses on note cards and photos of families who had been in our Sunday school class for the past seven years. Every day of the month was filled with a word of encouragement or a friendly face.

As my friend gave it to me, she said, "Put this in your new kitchen. Every day turn the page and know that you are loved and missed." That calendar was my lifeline my first few months in a new state. Sometimes, I would go through every page, every day. It brought me comfort that God would provide new friendships and create new memories that would bring a smile to my face.

That was eight years ago. I still have that calendar in my kitchen and I still look at it almost every day. It reminds me of the gift of friendship and the joy that comes from feeling as if you have a place where you belong.

If you know someone who is moving, provide a tangible link with their old home and its memories and friendships. Create a photo album, calendar, or collection of bon voyage cards to carry with them to their new home.

MOVING MADNESS!

Kim Erickson

MY HUSBAND AND I HAVE MOVED ACROSS THE COUNTRY FOUR TIMES so far. Each time our lives took a turn involving another grand adventure (this is how we think of it), our friends did something special for us. Their acts of kindness gave us hope that we would find new friends and build new memories in our new home.

If you know someone who is moving far away:

- Plan a special gathering in her honor before she leaves town.
- Create a picture collage of friends and memories.
- Find or create items with meaningful Bible verses.
- Find or create an item for her new home and include a note about your friendship.
- Provide some initial research on churches in her new city.
- Send a welcome home card to her new address so she has mail waiting when she arrives.
- Order a pizza online to be delivered to her new home after a long day of unpacking.
- Schedule time to talk on the phone, especially if there is a time difference.

Finally, be patient. Moving to a new city often creates "moving madness." Moving madness is caused by too many details to keep track of, not being able to find anything, and general crankiness because everything seems weird and unfamiliar. Your friend will need some time to come out of the madness!

Keep calling, keep emailing, and keep praying for her. Your acts of kindness will mean the world to her as she bravely faces her new adventure. Your thoughtfulness will fill her heart with the kind of hope that only friends can give to each other.

ENCOURAGING HOPE

Anonymous

THE MIDNIGHT PHONE CALL REMAINS FRESH IN MY MEMORY. Between heaving sobs, Sue groaned out, "Ricky murdered John."

Three years earlier, our church had an "adopt a single family" sign-up. I was excited to meet Sue and her almost two-year-old only child, John. John had an infectious enthusiasm for life, complete with an ear-to-ear smile and sparkling eyes that could warm any heart. He was everyone's "sunshine." A family celebration or holiday was not complete without John and Sue.

My prayers over the subsequent seven years always included, "Lord, how can I comfort Sue when I can't even begin to understand the great depths of pain she is enduring? Help me to extend Your unending love and hope to her." These are some of the practical ways God has led me to show Sue His love to give her hope.

- Send cards for no reason and include an encouraging Bible verse.
- Send cards that acknowledge a difficult time they are experiencing.
- Talk about the loved one and your memories.
- Go to coffee or lunch.
- Listen without judgment.
- Purchase Christmas or birthday gifts for the needy in honor of the victim; let the survivor know.
- Visit the gravesite and pray for the family suffering the loss; let the survivor know.
- Send texts or Facebook messages to encourage them.
- Name a pet in honor of them; we named a bird "Sunshine."
- Write an acrostic poem with the victim's name and give it to the survivor.
- Put something in your house that reminds you of the victim and pray for the survivor when you look at it. I have a "Sunshine" Care Bear on my kitchen windowsill.

SECURITY IN THE STORM

Andra Good

WHEN A TORNADO TORE THROUGH THE TOWN OF JOPLIN, MISSOURI, in 2011, my heart broke looking at the pictures of the devastation to the homes, schools, hospitals, and businesses. The news reported that the entire town had been wiped out, leaving many families with nothing. The Red Cross had moved in swiftly to provide food and water, and families found shelter in neighboring cities.

The thought of the young children involved in this tragedy broke my heart. What a traumatic experience to endure a storm of this magnitude, and then to lose everything you have at such a young age. I prayed for comfort for them and was then moved by the Lord to send them a small piece of security. Knowing that many of them had lost everything they owned, I realized they might have lost their personal blanket as well. A blankie provides comfort, warmth, and security, and during this experience I knew they could use that comfort.

I'm thankful to God that I learned of a man at a local church who was driving across the country the next morning to deliver a trailer full of goods for Joplin. He included eighty Leigh's Blankies (www. leighsblankies.com) in his trailer along with water, clothes, and other necessities donated by the community for the people of Joplin.

It was a blessing to see God's goodness leave in that trailer, and it was fulfilling to know the children in Joplin would receive God's love and security through a blankie. What tangible help can you offer to victims of natural disaster? Support your favorite disaster relief charity, and be alert to God's leading in how to offer help.

NEW JOB JITTERS

Kim Erickson

I HAVE WORKED FOR AT LEAST TEN DIFFERENT EMPLOYERS. THE ONE thing these jobs had in common was the fact that I started each one with new job jitters! When I start a new job, I feel insecure, unsure of myself, fearful of the unknown, and out of place. I wonder if I will fit in with the new team. I worry that I will not be able to perform in the way my new boss will expect. I forget any successes from previous jobs and focus on the "rookie" mistakes I am making in my new job. My new job jitters often took the joy out of the new opportunities God placed in my life.

If you know someone who is transitioning into a new job or switching to a new employer, you can bet she has her own new job jitters.

Here are some ideas to help her replace those worthless jitters with powerful hope for her new opportunity:

- Give her a list of her strengths to focus on during this transition.
- Find or create an encouraging item for her new office space.
- If you met this friend at a shared employer, remind her of how you met and how your friendship developed; remind her, too, that she will meet new friends at her new job.
- Together, create a list of reasons why this new job is a blessing from God.
- Encourage her to think of her new job as a new way for her to live out God's purpose for her life.
- Write Bible verses for her about God's purpose, plans, and provision.

MIRACULOUS MATTHEW

Adrienne Schiele

I REMEMBER THE NIGHT OF JUNE 8, 1993. I STARTED HAVING CON-tractions. Unfortunately, my baby was not due until August 24.

With a combination of reduced activity and medication, I made it a few weeks longer. However, within a few days of stopping medication my water broke, and Matthew Allen Schiele was on his way. It was scary to see my tiny premature baby hooked up to tubes and wires in an incubator in intensive care. I longed to hold him, but I wasn't allowed to.

I thanked God for the miracle of his very life, especially when the baby in the next incubator passed away.

Finally, we were able to bring Matthew home. I was grateful, but also afraid; he was tiny, barely five pounds. (My first baby had been nearly nine pounds and was very robust.)

The days were long and the nights even longer with a strict feeding and medication schedule. God enabled us to make it through. He provided my mother-in-law to help and church members to provide prayer and meals. My mother also came to assist and took over my household chores.

The strict feeding schedule paid off. Matthew more than doubled his weight by his two-month exam and was able to stop taking medication.

Today, Matthew is a healthy, grown man, thanks to God's grace and many who helped.

To support parents of a premature baby still in the hospital, visit if appropriate, supply change for vending machines, provide meals for the family, or offer to babysit other children. When the baby arrives home, ask if you can help with meals, house cleaning, laundry, running errands, grocery shopping, or feeding the baby so the mother can rest. And rejoice as the baby gains weight and grows!

HOPE AND LIFE

Bonnie Afman Emmorey

HOW DO YOU ENCOURAGE A FAMILY MEMBER WITH AN INCARCER-ated loved one? A "Hope Box" can brighten any day and bring the reminder that God loves and cares for them. Our ministry, Speak Up For Hope, provides them for friends who want to encourage a family with an incarcerated loved one. The Hope Boxes include one or more of the following items: an inspirational Christian book, a CD, coffee mug with flavored coffees or teas, bath and toiletry products, stationery, a candle and many other comfort items, plus a small Beanie Baby or another stuffed animal (like a lion, teddy bear, or lamb) peeking out of colorful crinkle-cut packaging with a card declaring encouraging words such as, "God knows your name" or "Be strong and courageous." Each box also contains a personal letter of encouragement to know that they have been prayed for personally.

How can you encourage an incarcerated loved one? Give them "A Slice of Life." My husband, Ron, writes our nephew, Jason Kent, every week in prison and sends pictures of the daily activities described in his letters. Jason calls it giving him "a slice of life." If you have children, have them draw pictures to send. They will be treasured. Statistics show that few prisoners have family members who continue to visit if the incarceration lasts longer than five years. If your loved one has a lengthy sentence or a life sentence, commit yourself to making regular visits for the duration.

You might also encourage someone who has been incarcerated to engage in a Bible study geared toward prisoners. Crossroads Bible Institute is one such ministry that offers guided instruction and personalized attention to prisoners. If you have a special heart for the incarcerated, you can even volunteer from home to check Crossroad Bible study lessons and write letters to encourage the incarcerated students.

"Remember those in prison as if you were together with them in prison, and those who are mistreated as if you yourselves were suffering" (Hebrews 13:3).

LOVE THROUGH PRAYER

Marlae Gritter

"Mom, do you remember those Scripture prayer notes that you always left on my pillow every Tuesday?" asked my former prodigal daughter.

"I sure do," I replied.

"What you never knew, Mom, is that during my prodigal years, every Tuesday night I cried myself to sleep because through those notes, I knew you still loved me, in spite of how rebellious and mean I was. And I still have every one!"

For many years, God had prompted me to write Scripture prayer notes for each of my children. I would place the note on their pillow every Tuesday, after I came home from meeting with my Moms in Prayer group. Isaiah 61:3 is what I often prayed for my prodigal. "Lord Jesus, I pray that You will bestow on _____ a crown of beauty instead of ashes, the oil of gladness instead of mourning, a garment of praise instead of a spirit of despair."

Are you feeling hopeless? Go to His Word, which is living and active! Pray His very words and believe that "He who began a good work in your child's life will see that it is finished" (cf. Philippians 1:6).

Never give up! God is working, according to His will, as you pray. It's the most powerful investment you can make. In His perfect time, His answer for your child will come. He wants to restore your hope!

And don't forget to write those little "love notes" of Scripture prayers. It's a wonderful way to say "I love you," and you will never know this side of heaven the hope they will also give to your prodigal.

SUPPORT GROUP FOR MOMS

LeAnne Gregory

WHEN YOU FIRST HOLD YOUR LITTLE CHILD IN YOUR ARMS, YOUR heart swells with joy and love. You want all the best of life for this little one. Time marches on, and the realities and disappointments of life show just how fragile is the human condition. Your child has grown cold to God, turned and walked away from Him, and there is nothing you can do about it. You need a Savior.

In Luke 15:4–7 we get a glimpse of the great love Christ has for those who've lost their way. We can relate this parable to Jesus, as the Good Shepherd, who came to seek and save those who are lost. In this we place our hope.

I experienced a season when my youngest son wandered away into dangerous territory. It was an agonizing time as a mother. There were many mothers in my church in the same situation, so one of them called us together to become a force in prayer for our children. We met regularly and prayed and shared God's promises with each other. One Christmas, the leader of our group gave each of us an ornament with a Bible promise for our prodigal. It was a symbol of hope and assurance. I still have the ornament, which reminds me that God keeps His promises.

My son's relationship with the Lord was restored! He is now married to a wonderful Christian woman and they have three boys.

If your child is wandering from the faith, look for other mothers who are suffering the same plight. Invite them to meet for prayer. Share a promise from God's Word. Share prayer requests. And pray.

Exchange a Christmas ornament with another mom and use it as a prayer prompter and symbol of hope. Believe God will fulfill His promises for your prodigal as He did for mine.

ACCEPTED!

Robin Johnson

REJECTION IN ANY FORM CAN BE DEVASTATING, ESPECIALLY TO women. It's hurtful when someone you respect or care about makes a comment or does something that feels like rejection to you. I place way too much value on human acceptance and affirmation.

My feelings are tossed back and forth with every comment or every action, and my day is often determined and defined by it. What would happen if I believed *truth*? That my Father God has given me everything I need? That all the treasures of wisdom and knowledge are in Him (Colossians 2:3)?

He has knit me together with strong ties of love. I don't have to fall apart every time another imperfect person touches my emotions with rejection. To be truthful, most times what that person says or does is more about their own insecurities and feelings of inadequacy than about me.

Today, I am choosing to believe the truth: I am loved, accepted, and forgiven by the God who created the universe! He defines me, not the world. If I don't allow Him to define me, I will allow everyone and everything else to do it. Be encouraged today and know God loves you! He has not rejected you and He never will:

- Know and believe who you are in Christ: loved, accepted, forgiven, a holy priesthood.
- Take captive every thought in obedience to Christ, replacing negative self-talk with the truth of God's Word.
- Allow God to affirm you daily.

A TIME TO WEEP
AND A TIME TO LAUGH

Kathe Wunnenberg

"IT'S OVER!" SOBBED MY FRIEND. "HE TOLD ME HE WANTS TO DATE other people."

No words could comfort my broken-hearted friend. I sat there and gave her permission to grieve. I plopped a box of tissues by her side and listened to her share her deep hurt and dashed hopes. I told her I was sorry for her loss. And I listened some more.

After a long afternoon of tears, I determined that she needed laughter. But what could I do? *God, help!* I prayed silently.

Then I remembered "Mr. Wonderful" tucked away in my closet. I bought him to spread hope and laughter to any woman struggling in a marriage or dating relationship. Standing only six inches high, this miniature man doll was tastefully dressed and sported an ear-to-ear grin. Moments later, I returned from the closet and handed him to my friend.

"Meet Mr. Wonderful!" I said.

My friend's bewildered look slowly transformed into a smile. Then she pressed the button on his chest.

With every word he spoke, her smile got bigger. Finally, she chuckled, then laughed, and I did too. I sent Mr. Wonderful home with her for a week and told her to keep him in her purse for a time to laugh after tears.

When someone you know experiences a breakup, give her permission to grieve her loss. Don't minimize her loss by saying, "You'll meet someone better." Listen. Let her express her hurt and disappointment freely. And when you think it's time, help her laugh again. The Bible says there is a time to weep and a time to laugh (Ecclesiastes 3:4). Be a friend for both seasons.

HOME FOR THE HOLIDAYS

Anne Denmark

CHRISTMAS FESTIVITIES WERE IN FULL SWING. THE WHOLE WORLD seemed caught up in the refrain of "Home for the Holidays." Meanwhile, a miscellaneous thought lodged in my mind.

I wondered what it would be like to no longer have the physical energy or mental agility to host a holiday gathering in your own home. What was it like when arthritic hands made meal preparation laborious and planning was beyond your grasp?

That stray thought wouldn't leave, so I invited eight seniors for a family dinner. The guests included those who recently lost their loved ones, a single who had never had the traditions of a family, and aging couples.

They arrived decked out in their Sunday best. Once comfortably seated in front of the fireplace, eyes brightened and tears of laughter ran down cheeks as they shared childhood memories.

I can still see the looks of disbelief on my children's faces as one gentleman shared that one year he only received a lump of coal in his stocking.

Stories continued around our dining table as we feasted on simple, comfort food of meat, potatoes, gravy, green beans, and warm rolls. We were family and we were home in Christ's love for the holidays.

As candles burned low, tender embraces closed that blessed evening. Years later ... those folks are now all in their heavenly homes and aging is beginning to slow my hospitality.

It refreshes my soul to watch my grown children inviting the single, the lonely, and the aging into their homes. What seniors need your home for the holidays?

LAUGHTER FOR LONELINESS

LeAnne Gregory

MY HUSBAND AND I MET AFTER A FEW YEARS OF BEING "SINGLE again" adults. We understand how lonely it can be not being a "couple," especially on Valentine's Day, one of the loneliest days in a single person's life. We thought about how we could alleviate the loneliness of the singles at our church. We decided to have an Enitnelav Yad party (Valentine Day spelled backwards) to take their minds off of it.

We asked them over for a mystery dinner at "Bonnie's Diner" (located in our living room and formal dining room). Dress for the night was anything crazy. The "mystery" was in the menu. The items on the menu were numbered and each was named by a riddle. This included their eating utensils; for example, "egg cradle" for spoon or "fluffy cloud" for mashed potatoes. Dinner consisted of three courses, six items for the first course, five items for the second, and five for the third. After the guests were seated at the tables, they were handed a menu and a paper with columns for each course and made their meal selections.

It was a lot of fun and certainly took their minds off of what day it was! What can you do to support the singles you know? Invite them along on family outings. Include them in a meal. Schedule regular get-togethers or coffee time. And offer practical help that they might miss receiving from a spouse, such as help with home repairs or cooking.

SUPPORTING INDEPENDENCE

Lori Walburg Vanden Bosch

MY FIFTY-THREE-YEAR-OLD SISTER, BETH, HAD TO MOVE. HER PRIvately run group home was closing, and with the help of Beth's social worker, my eighty-one-year-old mother began to look for a new place. Thankfully, in the matter of a month, we found a home with an opening. Better still, Beth already knew several of the residents because she worked with them at her special place of employment. We moved Beth's few belongings into the home, and she was warmly welcomed by her new roommate.

While each person with intellectual disabilities is different, I believe many of them share a desire for a degree of independence. As her four other siblings grew up and moved away, Beth too desired that change. Although intellectually she is at the level of a five-year-old, she enjoys her work, her friendships, and her unique hobby: collecting photos of RVs!

Churches play a key part in supporting the independence and dignity of those adults with special needs. I'm so grateful to churches with ministries for special needs adults, so they can enjoy fellowship and grow spiritually like any other Christian. I am grateful for Friendship Ministries, an organization that helps churches enfold and spiritually equip children and adults with intellectual disabilities.

But I am especially grateful to *individuals* who say hello to my sister, send Christmas and birthday cards, and listen patiently, even when the communication is garbled. With our dad now gone—someone who especially loved Beth—I treasure all the more the love from the body of Christ for people like her, a body that can enfold even its weakest members and celebrate their simple gifts.

WE'RE STILL (KINDA) NORMAL!

Linda Aalderink

WHO DEFINES WHAT NORMAL IS ANYWAY? ONCE I HEARD THE WORD described as a setting on a dryer. Most of the world today would define our family as something other than a normal family. Why? Because our oldest son has Down syndrome.

Our other two children have often been asked what they imagine their lives would be like if Zach had been born without special needs. Their response? This is normal for us. Having Zach a part of our family has not taken away "normal." It has enhanced us as a family, built a bond that is unique, and given us laughter and love beyond measure. Doesn't that sound normal? Actually, it is better than normal. Zach has taught us more about life than we have taught him.

I have been thankful for friends whose relationships with us didn't change because we have Zach in our family. In fact, I would submit that most of our family and friends would say getting to know Zach has actually blessed their family members with gifts of compassion and acceptance. There is so much to learn from Zach, and it's truly a privilege to journey life with him.

If you know a family with a special needs child, continue to engage with this family as you normally would. They need your friendship and the chance to feel like a typical family. Make the effort to get to know the special needs person. This will be a win/win for all. Ask God to show you activities for all family members to enjoy, including the special needs person.

SAFE IN THE ARMS OF JESUS

Debbie Kennedy

WHEN I WAS WORKING AT A MAJOR AIRLINE, I WAS OFTEN ASKED, "When are you going to have a baby?" Since I had been married for three years, everyone assumed that the time was coming soon. At that time, though, moving up the corporate ladder was my main priority.

One day, I was out of town on a business meeting and felt really tired. Before long, I confirmed the cause: I was twelve weeks pregnant. Surprise? Wow!

I had an uneventful pregnancy until one night I started having severe pain. I went to the emergency room and within minutes my water broke. What was going on? Within hours our son, Shane William Kennedy, was stillborn. He was so small and tiny, yet perfect in every way, down to his little hands and feet. The emotional pain that followed is indescribable. I went home empty-armed and broken-hearted.

Shortly after, my husband and I were at a mall, and he found a Precious Moments figurine. It was a baby angel sleeping on a cloud, named "Safe in the Arms of Jesus." This figurine brings us comfort each time I see it because Shane will forever be safe in Christ's strong arms.

A few of the most important things you can do when someone has an infant loss is to remember to always call the baby by name. Don't say, "I know how you feel." Even if it happened to you, each loss is different, and you may truly not know how they feel. Also, remember that the child will always be part of the family.

PAMPER STRESS AWAY

Kathe Wunnenberg

MY AUNT DON'S MILESTONE BIRTHDAY WAS FAST APPROACHING, AND I wanted to honor her. Since childhood, besides my parents, she was the one I counted on to "be there." Her special gifts, quality time, cards, and acts of kindness through the years ranked her as one of my favorite hopelifters.

During our long-distance phone call, she informed me, "I don't want any birthday cards!" I could tell she was anxious about this momentous occasion, so I prayed for creativity for the right gift. *Fly there!* God told me. I contacted my cousin Glenda, and we decided a weekend trip to Arkansas to see "Auntie" was the perfect gift.

For weeks, the three of us looked forward to our reunion. But when the weekend finally arrived, Glenda and I boarded the plane, both stressed. She had recently lost her job, and I was overwhelmed from balancing work, ministry, and life with three busy sons and a husband who traveled. Little did any of us know that the occasion causing Aunt Don's stress would be what God would use to reduce mine and Glenda's.

We gave our presence as a gift hoping to encourage her, only to receive far more than we gave. Aunt Don pampered our stress away with delicious meals, sightseeing, shopping, a private concert in her living room with her friend, Clay, and a surprise bath and massage at historic Hot Springs. And, of course, her famous cheesecake.

When someone is stressed over any circumstance, think of simple ways you could pamper her. Could your presence or a trip to see her help? Even if you can't send her to Hot Springs, you could offer a long, hot bath in your home, a hand massage, or even a cheesecake to pamper her stress away.

SOMEBODY'S STRESSED? GET PRACTICAL

Judith Couchman

WHEN I CREATED A NATIONAL WOMEN'S MAGAZINE, MANAGING IT from the idea stage through its launch into the world, I loved the project, but I feared I'd lose my mind or health (or both) from the stress. I logged sixty or more hours per week, grabbing every possible moment to chase deadlines. Consequently, I neglected personal details: errands begged for attention, housekeeping barely existed, and grocery shopping dwindled.

Friends and colleagues offered their (sometimes unwanted) time-management tips, work philosophies, books to read, and relaxation techniques. I didn't listen to most of it; their advice only stirred up more stress and lurking guilt. Then some friends got practical. On a snowy February day, three women formed a cleaning troop and stormed my house while I worked at the office. They packed up Christmas decorations, scrubbed bathroom scum, vacuumed neglected carpets, washed sticky dishes, cleaned out the refrigerator, and tackled anything that would make *Good Housekeeping* editors gasp. (One woman even visited the post office to purchase much-needed stamps.) The cost to me: a toothbrush somebody grabbed from the medicine cabinet to detail the bathroom sink fixtures.

Returning home that night, I felt enveloped in uncluttered peace and invigorated hope. With friends like this, I could muddle through my overwhelming, extended-stress life.

When people feel stressed, it's often the practical that helps most. Cook a meal, wash the dog, finish the laundry, babysit the kids, give a massage, clean anything, or volunteer as a one-day assistant. Offer hope in tangible, hands-on ways. Later on, that's what they'll remember.

BUCKET OF FAITH

Kathe Wunnenberg

WHEN I HEARD MY LONG-DISTANCE FRIEND, DARLENE, SUFFERED A stroke, I asked God to give me wisdom and creative compassion. During her early days of recovery, she was sedated and unable to receive calls. Prayer was my primary means of support. I left a voice message prayer on her husband's phone.

When I saw a purple comforter (her favorite color) in the store, I mailed it to her with a note: "God is your comforter."

As she recovered, I called more frequently. It was easier for her to listen than to speak. So I did most of the talking and limited my questions to "yes" and "no" answers. During one conversation, God prompted me to say, "Remember your bucket?"

I heard her chuckle. The "bucket" was our buzzword for faith. I had even mailed her a miniature silver bucket a few months earlier.

When Darlene was a child, she longed for an in-ground pool, but her father couldn't afford one. She told me about filling up a silver bucket with water and sitting in it in her backyard, thanking God for the pool He would someday give her.

One day, a man approached Darlene's dad to complete a project for him, but he didn't have the money to pay for it. Instead, he offered to trade services. Amazingly, he was a pool builder.

Darlene's bucket story of faith gave me hope through my own times of suffering and inspired me to have faith beyond what I could see. Her recovery from a stroke was just one more "bucket of faith." If you have a friend suffering from a stroke or other health challenge, remind her of specific instances of God's faithfulness to her in the past, as well as the truth that His mercies are "new every morning" (Lamentations 3:23). Great is His faithfulness!

A BASKET OF TISSUES

Kathe Wunnenberg

WHEN I GOT WORD MY FRIEND'S SON HAD DIED FROM SUICIDE, I WAS shocked. Although I was familiar with the experience of death and felt comfortable encouraging grieving moms, I had never experienced death by suicide. Uncertainty swept through my soul.

I had no idea the gut-wrenching pain my friend was experiencing, the guilt, the questions, the blame for somehow feeling she could have prevented it. I've been told by other mothers who have experienced loss through suicide that self-blame is a normal part of the grief journey.

All I knew is that my friend was in sorrow beyond her comprehension, and she needed God to be her Comforter.

Immediately, I went to the store to gather items for my usual gift for hurting people. I would give my friend permission to cry. The grocery clerk looked puzzled as I unloaded box after box of tissues in a variety of shapes and sizes.

"Is someone sick?" she asked.

"No, just hurting deeply and in need of a long cry," I said.

I headed to my friend's home armed with a broken heart and a wash basket filled with boxes of tissues, eye drops, a scented candle, and a simple card that read:

> "May God be your comforter and your light in the darkness.
> 'For the Lord comforts His people and will have compassion on
> His afflicted ones' (Isaiah 49:13b). 'Though I sit in darkness, the
> LORD will be my light' (Micah 7:8b)."

If someone you know has lost a loved one through suicide, pray for God to be her comforter and to protect her from self-blame or guilt. Invite the Holy Spirit to intercede for other unknown needs (Romans 8:26). Be sensitive to her sorrow beyond comprehension. Don't ask questions or give answers. Listen. God can shine through your presence or your tears as you sit with her in darkness.

HOPE BOARD

Kathe Wunnenberg

WHEN MY FAVORITE OUT-OF-STATE UNCLE WAS DIAGNOSED WITH Lou Gehrig's Disease, I had no idea what it was or how to encourage him. I discovered that his condition was terminal and would eventually destroy his ability to speak and walk. I cried out to God for creative compassion to be a hopelifter for Uncle June. A former postmaster and gregarious retiree, Uncle June's condition progressed quickly, and his frustration mounted as his speech slurred and diminished.

God used an ordinary trip to an office supply store to reveal to me a personalized plan of hope for Uncle June. In the checkout line, I spied a lap-sized whiteboard with dry-erase markers.

That's it! I thought.

Two days later, Uncle June opened up his cross-country surprise and chuckled when he read my note:

> *Dear Uncle June,*
> *You can still speak!*
> *Love,*
> *Kathe*

Uncle June loved his Hope Board. It became his new mode of communication. I enlisted my dad's support to help with Uncle June's Hope Board by keeping him supplied with dry-erase markers. Dad lived in the same town and visited Uncle June every day. He was faithful to bring hope to Uncle June by stopping by to see him, drink coffee, take him on car rides, and drive several miles to the next town to pick up markers. I'm grateful to Dad for being there for Uncle June when I couldn't be, and for modeling Jesus' heart of faithfulness and compassion to him through the years.

If you know someone facing a long-term, terminal illness, learn how the disease will affect the person. Pray for creative compassion. If you live far away, try to partner with someone who lives nearby to address that person's needs. If you are close, reach out with your personal presence. And pray!

BFFS FOR ALL ETERNITY

Alice Stephens

THERE'S NOTHING QUITE AS HURTFUL AS FINDING OUT YOUR BEST friend has terminal cancer. I met Suzanne at work in a new town and new job. I needed a good friend, and there she was with her big smile. She was also there when I married, and she was godmother when I had my son. Our friendship grew through the years. We trout fished together in mountain streams in Colorado, camped with our elk-hunting husbands, and shared family Thanksgivings. We developed a special bond.

When Suzie was diagnosed with terminal cancer, I was crushed. She was a giver, always seeing the needs of others and giving gifts she couldn't afford. Most of all, she gave of herself and was a friend to all who knew her. I decided now was the season to give back the love and concern she had always given me. Since she was hospitalized in the city where I lived, and later in a rehabilitation center nearby, I spent time after work with Suzie, recalling our past adventures, laughing, praying, and at times, just cradling her hand in mine when she was too ill to talk.

When Christmas was approaching, her room seemed dismal. I took a small lighted tree, baked lots of goodies, and decorated her room. She was thrilled and, being Suzie, I'm certain she shared goodies with staff and other patients. I realize the simplicity of my visits made a significant difference in her confined life.

If you know someone who is terminally ill, be with them as often as you can. Look for their needs and act to meet them. And give God's love—the only thing that cannot be swallowed up by death.

I look forward to seeing my friend, Susie, again, my BFF for all eternity.

PAY IT FORWARD

Anonymous

IN THE BEGINNING, ONE OF US WAS ON THE RECEIVING END OF A small act of kindness, and as they say, the rest was history.

We formed a small group of five anonymous women, each with a desire to shower other women with encouragement during a time of crisis. When one of us heard about someone from our church, neighborhood, or community who was going through a tough time with marital issues, financial problems, or perhaps just down in the dumps, we would contact the rest of the group with the particulars of ways we could provide encouragement.

We would devise a drop-off schedule so that the person would be surprised over the course of a week or so with small items being left at her door or sent in the mail by an anonymous sender. It could be anything from an encouraging card, a gift card, flowers, or a journal. Several times we would hear from various friends or others that this small act of kindness was just what the woman needed to become encouraged herself, and that our act had provided her with the desire to "pay it forward."

The signature calling card for our group was C.H.R.I.S.T., an acronym meaning Caring Helpers Reaching Individuals Sharing Treasures.

Perhaps you would like to become a member of a secret society of anonymous givers. If so, establish a small group of women who can keep a secret and have a willingness to encourage others. Keep your eyes and ears open for friends, acquaintances, and neighbors who are going through a time of crisis or who need encouraging. Get creative and leave small, thoughtful items. And remember, the gift is in the giving—anonymously.

SNOW DAY!

Janet Drez

FOR EIGHTEEN YEARS I HAD BEEN A BUSINESS OWNER, CREATED AND led business organizations, taught marketing classes at the local college, and served as a ministry volunteer. Without warning, things began to shift dramatically. Clients stopped calling, marketing efforts dried up, and God asked me to step down from being the chairwoman of the group He had led me to start. I felt the cut of His pruning and reeled. Things were rapidly transitioning in every area of my life.

During that season, I knew God was calling me to go deeper with Him, but the physical evidence of His hand and His working seemed nonexistent. I felt I had plunged into the cold, dark winter.

As I sat across from my friend, Kathe, pouring out my struggle, my confusion, and my winter analogy, she carefully listened and then laughed and said, "It sounds like you could use a snow day! Winter may seem dark and cold, but even in the midst there's the joy and fun of snow!"

My heart lightened and we laughed. One week later, we met again and Kathe handed me a snowflake ornament on which was written "Snow Day!" Then came an email with animated snowflakes and the message, "Thought you could use a Snow Day!" Throughout that dark season, Kathe would give me some reminder to savor snow days!

Thankfully, winter never lasts forever and transitions do end. When God had finished preparing me, spring arrived in the form of a life-changing ministry opportunity. Kathe was also the first to rejoice with me and to celebrate what God had done, but even now we'll occasionally stop to share a snow day.

If you know someone who is going through a time of transition, offer a listening ear, and if possible, a tangible reminder that God is with them through the changes.

EYES OF HOPE

Sofia Roitman Trillo

GRANDMA ALWAYS LOVED TO READ. RAISED IN A SMALL TOWN AND an avid reader since a young age, she read all the classic books available to her in the tiny library. Her best companions became her books, and she found her greatest comfort and hope in the Bible.

In 2004, as a very active grandmother of twenty grandchildren, she found herself suddenly unable to read her favorite stories to the grandkids who would crawl on her lap. Her vision became blurry, and within a few weeks she was unable to see. She couldn't even read her beloved Bible. An aggressive type of macular degeneration robbed her of her vision.

As I came to see her, I hardly recognized her. With tearful eyes, she lamented being unable to read, take care of herself anymore, or even stroll in her garden. She was heartbroken.

During the two weeks I visited, we enjoyed the warmth of the sunshine through her bedroom window and traveled in our imaginations all over the world as I read to her the classics of literature and encouragement from the Psalms of David.

As my time ended, I wondered how to keep Grandma's spirits high in the midst of long days full of darkness. Right then, a verse came to mind: "Your word is a lamp for my feet, a light on my path" (Psalm 119:105).

I rushed out to buy her a CD player, an audio Bible, and other audio books. She could now hear the beloved Word daily. If you know someone who is facing vision loss, offer a listening ear and loving companionship. Ask what activities are missed the most and search for a comparable replacement. Ask what kinds of music or books they enjoy, then buy or borrow CDs that will bless them.

LOSER BUDDY

Kathe Wunnenberg

THE PROBLEM OF OBESITY IS CLOSE TO MY HEART. SEVERAL PEOPLE I know struggle with their weight. Many have health issues beyond their control or take mandatory medication, with the side effect of weight gain. Too often, others judge them without knowing the problem behind their pounds.

Perhaps that's why the reality television series *The Biggest Loser* inspires me. It divides a group of overweight men and women into two teams, which celebrity fitness trainers oversee. Each week contestants engage in a rigorous nutrition and fitness regime. At the end of each episode, a weekly weigh-in determines which team has dropped the most pounds, and the losing group must send someone home. By the end of the season, one person, the biggest loser, wins.

Although I don't agree with everything on the program, I do think it has brought the growing problem of obesity to light and the increased need for health and fitness for everyone.

The show inspired a group of female coworkers to start a "biggest loser" challenge at work. Instead of getting personal trainers, they paired up as "loser buddies." Some met before work to pray. Others walked during lunch. They cheered each other on at the water fountain and swapped healthy recipes. At their weekly group meeting, they prayed and celebrated every success. They took time to listen and help those who failed to understand how to move forward the next week.

If someone you know is struggling with her weight, consider becoming her "loser buddy." Buddy her through prayer. Text "I'm praying for you" at mealtimes. Join her for a walk during lunch. Surprise her with a new water bottle with a label you create: "I can do all things through Christ who strengthens me" (Philippians 4:13). When she loses, celebrate!

WHY ME, LORD?

Nadia Brown

As I drove home with tears in my eyes, her words were on repeat in my mind. Another disastrous one-on-one with my manager had led me to the point of telling my husband I didn't want to go back. In all of my career, I don't think I've ever felt so horrible. I spent time that day crying out to God and asking why she was all over me and why we were constantly at odds. As I prayed and asked God to change her heart, promote her to another job—anything to get her away from me—He began to work on *my* heart and remind me that I was not in this alone.

"Love is patient, love is kind. It does not envy, it does not boast, it is not proud" (1 Corinthians 13:4). *What's love got to do with it?* I thought. Yet even while these thoughts ran through my mind, I knew I had to walk in love and forgive. Over the next several months, I spent time praying to God to touch my heart and help me walk in the love of Christ, no matter how my boss treated me. I also shared my concerns and frustrations on those days when I felt I couldn't bear it any longer. In time, she and I were able to reach a peaceful point, and soon after I moved on to a new role.

Is God looking to refine you through a workplace challenge? Open your heart and allow Him to work through you. Or if you know someone dealing with workplace issues, offer a compassionate, listening ear as she sorts through the problems and issues.

GOD BOX

Kathe Wunnenberg

ONE DAY DEBBIE'S MANAGER ANNOUNCED, "YOU'RE JOB IS BEING restructured." Although she couldn't control her circumstances, Debbie could control how she responded to them. She chose to trust God and believe He had a purpose and a plan.

A short time later, Debbie's mom became ill and was hospitalized. Tests revealed her mom had cancer with only a short time to live. Again, Debbie chose to trust God, believing He had a plan for her mom's care beyond the hospital. Friends rallied to join Debbie to pray.

Then Debbie discovered she would be losing her job. By losing this job, Debbie was now free to accept another: caregiver for her mom. Debbie brought her mom and two birds to her home to live her final days. Although her new job was sometimes filled with challenges and uncertainty, it also provided unexpected blessings and cherished memories with her mom. A few of us observed Debbie perform her most important job, being the hands and feet of Jesus to her mom. God's carefully orchestrated plan and perfect timing to provide this opportunity still amazes me.

When you or someone you know experiences workplace challenges, be willing to trust and believe that God has a purpose and a plan. Although His plan may not be obvious at first, be alert and make Jeremiah 29:11 your daily prayer. God *is* at work, even in difficulties. Often, a challenge may be a blessing in disguise. Thank God for your challenges; even if you don't feel thankful, do it anyway. Or, try this tip from Debbie's mom, Jackie: *write down your challenges on a piece of paper and put them in a God Box.* This needlepoint box with a lid, which Jackie made for me, reminds me to trust God. I use it often and think of my sweet friend, now in heaven. For every concern and challenge, God *does* have a plan. Trust Him. Grab any box. Write down your concerns. Place them in the box and release them to God. Then watch for God's plan at work.

(Write your own recipe here)

(Write your own recipe here.)

(Write your own recipe here.)

(Write your own recipe here.)

APPENDIX A

DISCUSSION GUIDE

How to Use This Guide

The following twelve lessons correspond to the first twelve chapters of this book and may be used in a variety of settings and time frames to meet your needs and spread hope.

You may choose to use them in a weekly series or weekend retreat to ignite fresh enthusiasm and vision for your ministry or organization and to spread hope to hurting people. Or you could use this as a timely training tool to encourage and equip your leaders and laypeople. Perhaps a more intimate setting with a small group, digging deeper together—in person or online—for six, eight, or twelve weeks may seem the right fit for you. Choose your setting and time frame. Do one or more lessons a week. This study guide may also be used as a comforting companion to guide you and a hurting friend over weekly coffee. Pray. Ask God to show you the right connections, setting, and time frame to help you grow and spread hope.

Lesson 1: Hopelifters Hope on Wheels

1. Read 2 Corinthians 1:3–4. How does this passage encourage you to live?

2. How do you see this truth demonstrated through the lives of women in the "bus story"?

3. Describe a time when someone comforted you and became the hands and feet of Jesus?

4. Take a few minutes to invite God to reveal someone to you who is hurting and needs hope.

5. Write down the person's name and greatest need on a three-by-five card.

6. Spend a few minutes "praising God" over that person (card) as the women did for Deborah in the bus story. Acknowledge God for who Scripture says He is and can be in that person's life: Healer, Comforter, Provider....

7. Invite God to give you a willing heart and ready hands to become a hopelifter and spread hope to hurting people this week.

Lesson 2: Knowing Hope

1. Read Ruth 1. How were Naomi and Ruth experiencing "no hope"? What did Ruth do to offer Naomi hope?

2. Share a time when a circumstance seemed hopeless, but God revealed His hope to you or through someone?

3. Read Jeremiah 14:8 and Psalm 119:81. How can you look eagerly ahead regardless of your circumstance and find and know hope?

4. Take a moment and focus your gaze on God Himself, who is your hope. Thank Him for loving you and caring about every detail of your life. Thank Him for His Word, His promises of hope.

5. If you're experiencing a season of suffering like Job (or know someone who is), what lessons can you learn from Job's life to show hope to other sufferers?

6. Invite God to help you be alert this week and look for ways He shows you hope in unexpected ways.

Lesson 3: Hope in a Person

1. Share your story of coming to know Jesus personally and receiving His free gift of eternal life. Thank God for the people He used in your journey to know Jesus.

2. Read the story in Mathew 15:32–39. How does this story encourage you? What is one small way you could meet a hurting person's physical needs?

3. How did Jesus meet the emotional needs of Mary after Lazarus died? What hidden hurt did He address in the Samaritan woman? How did He restore Peter after denying Him?

4. Jesus met spiritual needs by confronting sinners, teaching truth in a variety of ways, and defeating evil forces. Which approach do you feel the most comfortable with? How have you encouraged someone spiritually using this approach?

5. Invite God to increase your sensitivity this week to see those hurting physically, emotionally, or spiritually. Armor up and make Ephesians 6 your daily prayer.

Lesson 4: The Power Behind Our Hope

1. Read 1 Corinthians 3:16 and Ephesians 3:20. The Holy Spirit takes up residence in you. How does knowing His power is at work in you give you hope?

2. How do you know if you are relying on the Holy Spirit or your own strength? What do you need to do to surrender to live "Nothing but God" and be empowered by Him?

3. Share an example of how the Holy Spirit spoke to you through the Bible, through prayer, through circumstances, or through the church (people).

4. How did the story of praying for the solider and the "immeasurably more" bracelet encourage you to tap into the wonder-working power of the Holy Spirit, who magnifies our

efforts to spread hope to others? Invite the Holy Spirit to be your guide and teacher this week.

Lesson 5: Hope in a Place

1. What place or setting inspires you or brings you hope?

2. Home is a word that implies safety, comfort, and love. "None of us can feel hope unless we can feel a deep sense of being 'at home.'" What does this mean to you?

3. How did Brenda's story of offering her extra room and Erica's story of finding comfort in her Aunt Bonnie's home and friendship encourage you that hope can be found in a place?

4. Read Revelation 21:2–5; 22:1–5; and John 14:2. What excites you about your eternal home, heaven? Invite the Holy Spirit to reveal to you someone who needs to know Jesus and look forward to an eternal place of love, security, and rest. How could you be a hopelifter by opening your heart and perhaps even your home to that person?

Lesson 6: Hope in a Process

1. Read Romans 5:3–5. Based on these verses, what does S+P+C=H mean?

2. Where are you at in the process of hope today?

3. How did Kim's story of losing a child and starting a support group for grieving moms demonstrate hope in a process?

4. Share how a specific area of suffering in your life has come full circle and God is now using you to bring hope to others.

5. When God looks at a hurting person, anything is possible. How can you invite Him to open your life to His work to bring hope to others through each stage of hope?

Lesson 7: Hope in a Possession

1. Read Acts 4:32. How does this verse tell us to live as believers? What is the benefit of sharing our possessions?

2. Physical possessions may bring timely hope. How did Elijah receive hope from the penniless widow? How did God bless her faith and willingness to share?

3. What hidden, slightly used, or unused skills, talents, and life experiences do you have that could offer hope to others?

4. Believers are entrusted with spiritual gifts to serve, to build up the body of Christ, and to bring glory to God. What spiritual gift(s) has the Holy Spirit entrusted you with? How are you using it to spread hope to others? If you don't know, pray and ask God to show you, and ask other believers to share with you, what gift(s) they think you may have.

Lesson 8: Hope in a Connection

1. Read 1 Corinthians 12:26–27. What do these verses say about being connected to others?

2. Who did God connect to Saul (Paul), and how did each person do his/her part to help him?

3. How is hope "contagious"? How have people in the body of Christ brought hope to you in your life, and how were you inspired to pass it on to others?

4. Review the "Table of the Brokenhearted" story. How did hope spread in this story?

5. God knows how to link every hurting heart with a heart that can offer hope and healing. What is "your part"? How can God use it to give hope to someone this week?

Lesson 9: Overcoming Hope Blockers

1. Read Joshua 3. What external "hope blocker" did the Israelites face? What was God's command for them to overcome it?

2. Recall a time of suffering, success, or a circumstance in your life when your hope was blocked. How did God "cross you over" to hope again?

3. Picture yourself as one of the priests. What "internal obstacles" do you think they faced as they stepped forward?

4. Review Linda's airline ticket story. What internal and external obstacles did she and others face? How did the women respond to this hope blocker?

5. Read Joshua 4. What did the Israelites do to remember how God removed their hope blocker? Invite the Holy Spirit to remind you of the times God has removed your internal or external hope blockers and "crossed you over" to hope again. Write down each instance on an index card. When people ask, be ready to share.

Lesson 10: Hopelifters Need Hope Too

1. Why do you think God's directive in 1 Thessalonians 5:11 to "encourage one another and build each other up" is important?

2. Reflect on the issue of "self-care." What are intentional ways you can "fill your pitcher" so you are able to pour out hope to others?

3. Developing a network of support—"people before you, beside you, and behind you" and "wise advisors"—can keep you growing and help you spread more hope to others. Who are the people in your life in each category? In which category do you need the most support for this season of your life?

4. What significant role did Moses, Aaron, and Hur play in Joshua's ministry in Exodus 17:10–13?

5. Why is having a PIT Team important in your ministry as a hopelifter? Who are three people you could enlist to pray for you in your ministry to spread hope?

Lesson 11: Developing Your Hope Plan

1. Review Sandy's story. Why do you think it's important to prepare your heart before you reach out to someone who is hurting?

2. "Lord, break my heart with what breaks yours." What does this mean to you?

3. It's time for a hope audit. What tangible resources or physical possessions can you offer? What intangible resources (spiritual gifts, talents, skills, connections, expertise, life experiences) are entrusted to you by God so that you can serve others?

4. Why is it important to evaluate the role of time in your hopelifting and your lifetime commitments?

5. Pray for creativity. Ask God to help you personalize your hope plan and point others to Jesus through it. Look through the recipes of hope in the previous pages and share your favorite one. Or, write one of your own on a blank recipe page included in this book and share it with your group.

Lesson 12: Spreading Your Hope

1. Share creative ways you've experienced "hope spreading" during this study.

2. How did Crystal's story and "surprise wedding" inspire you that "even in the midst of suffering, hope lives"? Who were Crystal's hopelifters? What kind of hope did they give her?

3. Review the section on Future Hope. Which example to spread hope to future generations inspired you most? How are you investing in spreading a legacy of hope?

4. Investing in Jesus, the chief Hopelifter, is an investment that continues to spread and give hope. How have you been inspired by this study to be a hopelifter and to spread hope to others?

5. Read Revelation 19:1–10. Imagine the day Jesus returns as our bridegroom to take us who know and love Him—*His church*— as his bride, to celebrate the eternal wedding.

6. List the names of people you know who have not accepted Jesus as their Lord and Savior or you're uncertain if they have:

Eternal Wedding Invitation List

_____	_____	_____
_____	_____	_____
_____	_____	_____
_____	_____	_____

Pray for the people on your list to have a pure and willing heart (Ps. 51:10-12) and ears to hear (Rev. 3:6): *Open _____'s eyes and turn him/her from darkness to light, and from the power of Satan to God, so that he/she may receive forgiveness of sins and a place among those who are sanctified by faith in Jesus.* (From Acts 26:18)

Pray for God to work through you to share creative compassion as Jesus' hands and feet until He returns. Keep spreading hope, dear friend and hopelifter. I'll look forward to seeing you and the people on your list at the wedding!

VERSES OF HOPE

"He sent out His word and healed them."
—PSALM 107:20

It only takes a moment to share God's Word with someone in need of timely hope. The following verses are favorites of hopelifters who were hurting and found comfort in God's Word. Choose one or more and share them in a card, text, email, or voice message, or as a personalized prayer for someone.

Trust in the LORD with all your heart
    and lean not on your own understanding;
in all your ways acknowledge Him,
    and He will make your paths straight.

PROVERBS 3:5–6

"For I know the plans I have for you," declares the LORD, "plans to prosper you and not to harm you, plans to give you hope and a future. Then you will call on Me and come and pray to Me, and I will listen to you. You will seek Me and find Me when you seek Me with all your heart."

JEREMIAH 29:11–13

I called on your name, LORD,
    from the depths of the pit.
You heard my plea: "Do not close Your ears
    to my cry for relief."
You came near when I called You,
    and You said, "Do not fear."

LAMENTATIONS 3:55–57

Therefore, with minds that are alert and fully sober, set your hope on the grace to be brought to you when Jesus Christ is revealed at His coming.

1 PETER 1:13

Look to the LORD and His strength;
    seek His face always.

PSALM 105:4

The LORD will guide you always;
    He will satisfy your needs in a sun-scorched land
    and will strengthen your frame.
You will be like a well-watered garden
    like a spring whose waters never fail.

ISAIAH 58:11

Forget the former things;
    do not dwell on the past.
See, I am doing a new thing!
    Now it springs up; do you not perceive it?
I am making a way in the wilderness
    and streams in the wasteland.

ISAIAH 43:18–19

The LORD is my strength and my shield;
    my heart trusts in Him, and He helps me.
My heart leaps for joy,
    and with my song I praise him.

PSALM 28:7

And the God of all grace, who called you to His eternal glory in Christ, after you have suffered a little while, will Himself restore you and make you strong, firm and steadfast.

1 PETER 5:10

Cast all your anxiety on Him because He cares for you.

1 PETER 5:7

The LORD is a refuge for the oppressed,
    a stronghold in times of trouble.
Those who know Your name trust in You,
    for You, LORD, have never forsaken those who seek You.

PSALM 9:9–10

How precious to me are your thoughts, God!
    How vast is the sum of them!
Were I to count them,
    they would outnumber the grains of sand—
    when I awake, I am still with You.

PSALM 139:17–18

Do not fear, for I have redeemed you;
    I have summoned you by name; you are Mine.
When you pass through the waters,
    I will be with you;
and when you pass through the rivers,
    they will not sweep over you.
When you walk through the fire,
    you will not be burned;
    the flames will not set you ablaze.
For I am the LORD your God,
    the Holy One of Israel, your Savior.

ISAIAH 43:1–3

The Lord is close to the brokenhearted
    and saves those who are crushed in spirit.

PSALM 34:18

Let your gentleness be evident to all. The Lord is near. Do not be anxious about anything, but in every situation, by prayer and petition, with thanksgiving, present your requests to God. And the peace of God, which transcends all understanding, will guard your hearts and your minds in Christ Jesus.

PHILIPPIANS 4:5–7

He replied, "Because you have so little faith. Truly I tell you, if you have faith as small as a mustard seed, you can say to this mountain, 'Move from here to there,' and it will move. Nothing will be impossible for you."

MATTHEW 17:20

He will cover you with His feathers,
   and under His wings you will find refuge;
   His faithfulness will be your shield and rampart.

PSALM 91:4

Be strong and courageous. Do not be afraid or terrified because of them, for the LORD your God goes with you; He will never leave you nor forsake you.

DEUTERONOMY 31:6

Now to Him who is able to do immeasurably more than all we ask or imagine, according to His power that is at work within us, to Him be the glory.

EPHESIANS 3:20

Finally, be strong in the Lord and in His mighty power. Put on the full armor of God, so that you can take your stand against the devil's schemes. For our struggle is not against flesh and blood, but against the rulers, against the authorities, against the powers of this dark world and against the spiritual forces of evil in the heavenly realms. Therefore put on the full armor of God, so that when the day of evil comes, you may be able to stand your ground, and after you have done everything, to stand. Stand firm then, with the belt of truth buckled around your waist, with the breastplate of righteousness in place, and with your feet fitted with the readiness that comes from the gospel of peace. In addition to all this, take up the shield of faith, with which you can extinguish all the flaming arrows of the evil one. Take the helmet of salvation and the sword of the Spirit, which is the word of God.

EPHESIANS 6:10–17

HELPFUL, HOPEFUL WEBSITES FOR CARING

www.hopelifters.com Hopelifters provides resources, tools, and more recipes of hope.

www.caringbridge.org Caring Bridge is a health social network to keep family, friends, and supporters connected. Anyone with a health care issue can create a personalized Caring Bridge website.

www.stephensministry.org Stephens Ministries is a resource and training organization that equips laypeople to provide one-on-one Christian care to hurting people.

www.mendingthesoul.org Mending the Soul is a training organization that empowers the church for ministry to those impacted by abuse.

www.celebraterecovery.org Celebrate Recovery is a Christian twelve-step program based for people with hurts, habits, and hang ups, including sex disorders or drug and alcohol addictions.

www.griefshare.org Grief share is a Christian grief support program.

www.speakupforhope.org Speak up for Hope provides hope to prisoners and their families through resources and encouragement.

www.cbi.fm Crossroad Bible Institute provides free Bible studies to prisoners and equips the church to enlist volunteers to help check the lessons.

www.friendship.org This ministry helps individuals and churches minister spiritually to the intellectually disabled.

www.momsinprayer.org Moms in Prayer is an international ministry of women praying for their children and schools. Their website provides prayer tools and resources.

www.younglife.org Young Life is an international ministry that introduces adolescents to Jesus Christ and helps them grow in their faith.

www.focusonthefamily.org Focus on the Family is a ministry that helps families thrive.

www.hannah.org Hannah's Prayer provides Christian support for fertility challenges, including infertility and the loss of a child from conception to birth.

www.dc4k.org Divorce Care for Kids helps children heal from the pain of divorce.

www.joniandfriends.org Joni and Friends provides resources and support to people with disabilities and their families.

www.speakupconference.com The Speak Up Conference provides training for Christian speakers, writers, and leaders.

www.teenchallengeusa.com A nationwide residential program providing youth, adults, and families with an effective and comprehensive Christian faith-based solution to life-controlling drug and alcohol problems in order to become productive members of society.

NOTES

1. Larry Richards, *Zondervan Expository Dictionary of Bible Words* (Grand Rapids: Zondervan, 1991), 344.

2. Ibid., 633.

3. Jim Cymbala, *Fresh Wind, Fresh Fire* (Grand Rapids: Zondervan, 2003), 152.

4. Ibid.

5. Larry Richards, *Zondervan Expository Dictionary of Bible Words*, 362.

6. Jim Cymbala, *Fresh Wind, Fresh Fire*, 148–49.

7. Henry Blackaby, *Experiencing God: Knowing and Doing the Will of God* (Nashville: Lifeway, 1990), 77.

8. For more on heaven, see Isaiah 35:10; 65:17; Ezekiel 1:26–28; Luke 15:10; John 3:5–7; 14:2–3; 1 Corinthians 15:35–38; Philippians 3:20–21; 1 Thessalonians 4:16–17; 2 Timothy 4:8; Hebrews 12:22–23; and Revelation 15:2–3; 20:1; 22:5.

9. Randy Alcorn, *Heaven* (Wheaton, Ill.: Tyndale, 2004), 17–18.

10. Carol Travilla, *Caring without Wearing: A Small Group Discussion Guide* (Colorado Springs, CO: NavPress, 1990). Carol later wrote, with Joan Web, *The Intentional Woman: A Guide to Experiencing the Power of Your Story* (Colorado Springs, CO: NavPress, 2002).

11. Carol Kent, *Becoming a Woman of Influence: Making a Lasting Impact on Others* (Colorado Springs, CO: NavPress, 1999), 112.

CONTRIBUTORS

Meet and connect with fellow hopelifters, the contributors to Recipes of Hope. Go to www.hopelifters.com to discover more about the contributors.

Linda Aalderink is a speaker and the author of *Immeasurably More: More Hope, More Joy: Embracing Life with Down Syndrome*. A mom of three, she lives in Michigan with her husband of over 30 years. See www.LindaAalderink .com

Starr Ayers is a third-generation artist, writer, and speaker living in North Carolina. As the mother of a daughter with Down Syndrome, her heart is to encourage the acceptance of those with life-challenging disabilities and to inspire others to embrace their own uniqueness. See http://365degreelens .blogspot.com.

Robyn Bellerson has been an educator, teaching in both public and private Christian schools for the past 20 years. She is a native to Arizonia, still residing in Chandler, Arizona, with her husband, Dave, and two teenage children.

Nadia Brown is a coach, facilitator, and writer who helps women discover and develop their natural leadership skills and abilities. She is the founder of Doyenne Leadership Institute and lives in Phoenix, Arizona, with her husband. See www.doyenneleadership.com.

Erica Carlson is a special education teacher who loves being a military wife and encouraging other military wives. She lives in Sparta, Michigan, with her husband, a second lieutenant in the Marine Corps.

Gia Chapman lives in Chandler, Arizona, and is a wife and busy mom to five living children (one through adoption). After losing her infant daughter, Sable Marie, she and her family started Sable's Wings, a nonprofit ministry supporting grieving families. See www.sableswings.org.

CONTRIBUTORS

Sharon Cochran encourages others to walk by faith. Through the experience of her son's catastrophic injury, she is building awareness to youth athletes and their parents about protection from head injuries. She is a businesswoman, wife, and busy mom to three, who lives in Phoenix, Arizona.

Judith Couchman is an author, international speaker, and adjunct art history professor. She's published more than forty books, Bible studies, and compilations, including *The Art of Faith*, *The Mystery of the Cross*, and *Designing a Woman's Life*. See www.judithcouchman.com.

Lisa DeLight is a speaker, writer, and performer. She practices love and hospitality as the general manager of Living Water Retreat Center in Cornville, Arizona. Her personal heroes are her four daughters. See her website, http:\\lisadelight.wordpress.com.

Anne Denmark, a Certified Professional Coach, supports people in living out their God-given purpose. Anne serves on the faculty of the Professional Christian Coaching Institute and trains participants at the Speak Up Conference with Carol Kent Ministries. Anne and her husband live in Tucson, Arizona. See www.lifediscoverycoaching.com.

Janet Drez is a speaker, author, Bible teacher, women's ministry director, and the founder of Octopus Faith (www.octupusfaith.com). She enthusiastically encourages women to grow deeper with God and become all he intends them to be. Janet is married to her high school sweetheart, and they have two young adult children.

Brenda Dull opens her home to Christian women in need of replenishment and to four-legged friends in need of her pet-sitting service, Prayer Paws. She lives in Chandler, Arizona, with her two dogs, Honey and Bear.

Bonnie Afman Emmorey is the Director of Speak Up For Hope, a nonprofit organization, giving hope and encouragement to prisoners and their families (www.speakupforhope.org). She is also the Administrator for The Speak Up Conference (www.speakupconference.com). Bonnie is blessed with a husband and two grown sons.

Kim Erickson is a passionate Bible study teacher and writer. After losing her three-year-old son, her sense of urgency ignited to help women study God's Word and grow (www.FindYourWayMinistries.org). She lives with her husband and living son in Jacksonville, Florida.

Brenda Evans is a former educator and curriculum development writer. She is currently working on a young adult mystery and a series of children's books. She resides in Chandler, Arizona.

Mary Jane Farr manages nonprofit and LLC corporations and coaches individuals in business and ministry with her husband through National Consulting Services. As licensed facilitators, they train leaders in The Prepare/Enrich Program and LifePlan. They serve on the advisory leadership council of Marriage Ministry at Scottsdale Bible Church in Arizona.

Andra Good is the founder and director of Leigh's Blankies, a nonprofit organization committed to making and distributing blankies to children in need worldwide. She lives in Gilbert, Arizona, with her husband and two daughters. See www.leighsblankies.com

Linda Grabeman is the author of *No Prissy Shoes*, a 31-day devotional for women walking through breast cancer. After walking this hard journey herself, she now encourages women with cancer to live with faith and joy, regardless of their circumstances. See www.noprissyshoes.com.

Marlae Gritter is the Executive Vice President of Moms in Prayer International, a ministry of mothers who pray for their children and schools (www.momsinprayer.org). She speaks and trains globally on how to develop your personal prayer life. Marlae lives in Holland, Michigan, with her husband. They have three adult children and three grandchildren.

LeAnne Gregory shares Christ's joy with others through her music, art, and writing. She has led worship for several Hopelifter events. LeAnne lives in Clarkdale, Arizona, with her husband. They have a blended family of six grown children, eleven grandchildren, and one great grandchild.

Tanya Glanzman is a speaker and writer known for her ability to offer hope and encouragement wrapped in grace-filled truth. She is the founder of My Father's Daughter Ministries (www.myfathersdaughter.com). She lives in Virginia with her husband and two children.

Alonna Hoogesteger, RN, is a certified Christian life purpose coach and grief facilitator, speaker, and writer. Her uplifting and inspiring messages encourage women whose journeys have been marked with pain, grief, and loss. She lives in Port Edwards, Wisconsin, with her family.

CONTRIBUTORS

Karen Howells is a mother, executive coach, wife, business owner, consultant, and writer always looking for opportunities to make a difference in others' lives. A native Oregonian, Karen finds life in her fifties is a new adventure in faith, growth, and purpose. See www.thehowellsgroup.com.

Barbara Hunsaker has been an educator for more than twenty-nine years. She is currently the principal of Bethany Christian School in Tempe, Arizona. She lives in Gilbert, Arizona, with her husband and their two college-age sons.

Robin Johnson is an honest, transparent creative writer who lives in Tempe, Arizona with her husband. They have three adult children and two grandsons. Read her story of redemption and scandalous grace at www .robin-johnson.com.

Erinn Kanney is called to be a "Restorer of Hope" to those who have suffered loss. Her dream is to create "Camp Eric," a place for people to experience restoration in Christ. Erinn lives in California and works with people with developmental and psychological disabilities.

Debbie Kennedy is passionate about encouraging grieving people. A former Bible study and support group leader for women who lost children, she currently helps with funerals and hospital visitation at her church and with Hopelifters' bus trips for grieving moms. Debbie lives in Gilbert, Arizona, with her husband and three living children.

Lisa Kowalski is the founder of Beloved Ministries and the faith-based True Beauty Tours: *Living like a Divine Princess in a Diva-like World*. She is passionate about living out her femininity, becoming an intentional woman God can use, and celebrating life, family, and friendship.

Rachel Lewis is a writer, speaker, and youth mentor. She is passionate about speaking to youth about sexual purity and missions. She lives in Cornville, Arizona, with her husband, and loves her new role as mom. See rachelrlewis.wordpress.com.

Diane Meehl's highest calling is to serve, inspire, and showcase people through the written word. An independent copywriter, journalist, and editor, she and her family make their home in Phoenix, Arizona. Her work has appeared in numerous publications, and her contributions to the column, "The Spiritual Side," can be found at www.ahwatukee.com.

Becky J. Miller is a writer, Moms in Prayer group leader, wife, mom to two grown sons, and an Army veteran, having served six years receiving the rank of captain. She encourages people to apply their faith in practical, everyday situations at www.godslemonadestand.blogspot.com.

Donna Morris works at JPMorgan Chase Bank and is a wife, mother, daughter, sister, aunt, friend, and lover of animals. She lives in Phoenix, Arizona, with her husband, son, and black Labrador, Odie.

Louise Nichols is a writer, teacher, and public speaker who is passionate about teaching God's Word to people seeking a deeper relationship with Him. The author of *Reassigned: Evil's Thief*, Louise lives in Gilbert, Arizona, with her husband and daughter, awaiting the arrival of another daughter from China.

Deb Niehof is the wife of a retired pastor and mother of three adult children. A former educator, she now directs a local affiliate of the National Alliance on Mental Illness, providing education and support to individuals living with mental illness and their family members. See www.nami.org.

Karen Lynn Ray is a licensed and certified associate counselor in Arizona. She provides biblically based psychotherapy for both couples and individuals through Abundant Hope Counseling Center. She lives in Phoenix, Arizona, with her husband and three sons.

Kim Slaughter is a support group leader and a small business owner. Known for her compassion and care for hurting people, she is the co-founder of a support group at her church for the loss of a baby. She lives in Gilbert, Arizona, with her husband.

Adrienne Schiele is a praying wife and mother. She embraces everyday situations to relate to others and give them God's encouragement. She lives in Chandler, Arizona, and enjoys camping and riding all-terrain vehicles with her family.

Alice Stephens is a mother, grandmother, great-grandmother, neighbor, and friend. Even with declining health, she stays busy encouraging others, writing, listening, and praying. She is a member of Kathe's PIT Team and lives in the foothills of the Ozarks in Missouri.

Sofia Roitman Trillo is an author and illustrator bringing hope to hurting children. She's the co-founder of Fun with a Message, a publishing company promoting books to encourage children with positive life lessons. She lives in Phoenix, Arizona, with her husband and daughter. See www .funwithamessage.com.

Lori Walburg Vanden Bosch is a freelance editor and author of the Christian children's picture books *Legend of the Candy Cane* and *Legend of the Easter Egg*. She lives in Grand Rapids, Michigan, with her husband and two children. She encourages you to check out Friendship Ministries for the intellectually disabled at www.friendship.org.

Shayla Van Hofwegen is the founder/director of Owl Love You Forever, a nonprofit organization donating hope boxes to hospitals for families who've lost a baby (www.owlloveyouforever.org). Her blog, *Wegen Tales*, encourages women experiencing infertility or the loss of a baby. She lives in Buckeye, Arizona, with her husband and adopted daughter.

Shelly Watkins is a budding author and Bible study teacher, with a heart for serving in her husband's ministry, women's ministries, missions, and community outreach. She lives in West Frankfort, Illinois, with her husband and is a homeschooling mom to their five children.

Erica Wiggenhorn is a speaker, author, and passionate Bible teacher inspiring women to apply Scripture's truth and fulfill their God-given calling. The author of *Ezekiel, Every Life Positioned for Purpose*, Erica resides in Litchfield Park, Arizona, with her husband, and their two children. See www.EricaWiggenhorn.com.

Charity Worden is a worship pastor, drama, and music teacher, wife, and mother of six living in Lake Montezuma, Arizona. She also writes scripts and readings to creatively facilitate worship experiences.

AUTHOR'S NOTE

Dear Friend,

Thank you for getting on board to journey with me through my book. I pray God has met you in the stories and enlarged your perspective of hope. Isn't it exciting to know God can use a person, place, process, possession, or connection to bring hope, and *anything* you offer Him can be transformed and used to spread hope to hurting people?

As I finish this letter, I'm sitting at my desk looking at a picture on my wall called "The Sower." It shows Jesus' nail-pierced hand spreading seed in a field. Every day during my writing journey, I've looked at this picture, and it's prompted me to pray for you. I've asked God to use my seeds of suffering through my life and in this writing process to bring you hope in a personal way. I've also prayed God would use *you* to be the hands of Jesus and spread seeds of hope to those in need.

I'd love to hear how God's power is at work in your life and the creative ways you are being a hopelifter for Him. Take a moment and let me know.

Keep growing, dear friend. Stay close to Jesus and keep sharing His love. May His hope be contagious and spread to others, who spread it to others, who spread it to others ... like wildflowers!

His hopelifter and yours,

KATHE (Proverbs 3:5–6)
www.hopelifters.com
Also on Facebook and Twitter

ABOUT THE AUTHOR

Kathe Wunnenberg is a hopelifter. She believes God can use *anything* you offer Him—a place, possession, connection, or personal life experience—and transform it into a meaningful resource of hope for someone in need that can be multiplied.

Known for her visionary leadership, creativity, and compassion-in-action lifestyle, Kathe is a communicator and connector who loves to offer biblical solutions and practical resources for real-life problems. God has sustained her through numerous life challenges, including infertility, adoption, miscarriages, carrying a child with a fatal birth defect, the loss of a child, parenting extreme children, depression, and starting, leading, and leaving a ministry.

Kathe is the author of *Grieving the Loss of a Love One, Grieving the Child I Never Knew, Longing for a Child,* and *Hopelifter: Creative Ways to Spread Hope When Life Hurts.*

She is the founder and president of Hopelifters Unlimited and lives in Phoenix, Arizona with her husband and three living sons. To learn more, connect with Kathe at www.hopelifters.com, or follow her on Facebook or Twitter @hopelifters.

HOPELIFTERS
UNLIMITED

Hopelifters Unlimited was founded in 2005 and is a Christ-centered organization dedicated to spreading hope in the world.

We are founded on the principles in Romans 5:3-5; 2 Corinthians 1:3-5; Jeremiah 29:11; Proverbs 3:5-6; and Isaiah 61.

For information on our current resources and the variety of ways Hopelifters Unlimited can encourage you, go to:

www.hopelifters.com

Grieving the Loss of a Loved One

Kathe Wunnenberg

Another book by Kathe Wunnenberg, to encourage anyone who has lost someone they love ...

The bottom has dropped out of your life. Will the ache ever cease, the tears ever stop?

How can you go on in the face of a grief so profound?

Kathe Wunnenberg knows the terrible pain of losing your loved one and she understands that the sense of loss never really goes away. Yet as surely as God is faithful, there is hope for your broken heart to mend. There is life beyond the sorrow. As hard as it might be to believe right now, there is even the promise of joy in due season as you walk through your grief one day at a time.

Grieving the Loss of a Loved One is a collection of devotions especially for you, especially for now. You will find this book to be a wise, understanding, and comforting companion to help you grieve in the ways you must, and to encourage you that God has not forsaken you.

- Includes a Scripture passage and prayer for each devotion
- Offers readings for holidays, birthdays, and special occasions
- Provides space for journalizing after each devotion

Available in stores and online!

Grieving the Child I Never Knew

Kathe Wunnenberg

"A tender and helpful book leading those who grieve over the death of an unborn child to the help they seek."

—ELISA MORGAN

When the anticipation of your child's birth turns into the grief of miscarriage, tubal pregnancy, stillbirth, or early infant death, no words on earth can ease your loss. But there is strength and encouragement in the wisdom of others who have been there and found that God's comfort is real.

Having experienced three miscarriages and the death of an infant son, Kathe Wunnenberg knows the deep anguish of losing a child. *Grieving the Child I Never Knew* was born from her personal journey through sorrow. It is a wise and tender companion for mothers whose hearts have been broken — mothers like you whose dreams have been shattered and who wonder how to go on.

This devotional collection will help you grieve honestly and well. With seasoned insights and gentle questions, it invites you to present your hurts before God and to receive over time the healing that He alone can — and will — provide.

Each devotion includes:

- Scripture passage and prayer
- "Steps Toward Healing" questions
- Space for journaling
- Readings for holidays and special occasions

Available in stores and online!

ZONDERVAN®
.com

Share Your Thoughts

With the Author: Your comments will be forwarded to the author when you send them to *zauthor@zondervan.com.*

With Zondervan: Submit your review of this book by writing to *zreview@zondervan.com.*

Free Online Resources at
www.zondervan.com

Daily Bible Verses and Devotions: Enrich your life with daily Bible verses or devotions that help you start every morning focused on God. Visit www.zondervan.com/newsletters.

Free Email Publications: Sign up for newsletters on Christian living, academic resources, church ministry, fiction, children's resources, and more. Visit www.zondervan.com/newsletters.

Zondervan Bible Search: Find and compare Bible passages in a variety of translations at www.zondervanbiblesearch.com.

Other Benefits: Register to receive online benefits like coupons and special offers, or to participate in research.